CODING

for Kids
2019 EDITION

Publisher and Creative Director: Nick Wells
Project Editor: Polly Prior
Assistant Editor: Josie Mitchell
Art Director and Layout Design: Mike Spender
Layout Design: Jane Ashley
Digital Design and Production: Chris Herbert
Copy Editors: Katharine Baker and Anna Groves
Screenshots and Technical Editor: Adam Crute
Proofreader: Dawn Laker
Indexer: Amanda Leigh

FLAME TREE PUBLISHING
6 Melbray Mews
London SW6 3NS
United Kingdom

All non-screenshot images are courtesy of Shutterstock and © the following: 1, 97, 211 Ollyy; 3, 22, 253 Syda Productions; 4, 14 LITUSPRO; 5, 20, 36, 42, 78, 108, 110, 123 Rawpixel.com; 5, 62, 188 Allies Interactive; 6, 7, 152, 198 Melpomene; 8 Uber Images; 16 garagestock; 19 Alena Ozerova; 21 Lina Truman; 22 Rvector; 23 Ionut Catalin Parvu; 25 EgudinKa; 26 Julia Kaysa; 28 My Life Graphic; 30 agshinrajabov; 30 Ilike; 31, 222 Zurijeta; 33 Angela Waye; 34 Arpan Rank; 37 Bloomicon; 38 PureSolution; 39 Yurich; 43 xtock; 47 cosmaa; 50 Julia Tim; 52, 64 gdainti; 58 rvlsoft; 64 Dragon Images; 65 (b) jamie cross; 65 (t) RedKoala; 66 Brian A Jackson; 67 Shai_Halud; 68 magic pictures; 75 rvlsoft; 77, 161, 164, 167 BEST-BACKGROUNDS; 80 bearsky23; 81 Grishankov; 81 sumroeng chinnapan; 90 Jane Kelly; 91 T. Lesia; 92 Abscent; 93 VoodooDot; 94 Mascha Tace; 96 issumbosi; 102 PrinceOfLove; 103 Studio_G; 103 antoniodiaz; 121 Sergey Maksienko; 126 art_of_sun; 134 filborg; 136 Africa Studio; 141 Chomon; 147 vasabii; 149 venimo; 155 M Studio; 158 Danielala; 163 gonin; 165 arrowsmith2; 166 Africa Studio; 170 Creative Stall; 172 Andrew Paul Deer; 173 Orkhan Naghiyev; 174 Monkey Business Images; 175 VectorsMarket; 176 Andrey_Popov; 179 spainter_vfx; 182 Evgeny Bornyakov; 184 Run The Jewels; 193 Maksim M; 196 Kit8.net; 197 Dragon Images; 205 Christos Georghiou; 207 matrioshka; 212 Wildjohny; 213 sakkmesterke; 216 Valua Vitaly; 217 studiostoks; 219 Radiocat; 221 Fred Mantel; 226 iunewind; 227 Khakimullin Aleksandr; 230 Anna Panova; 238 Jaroslav Machacek; 243 Jacek Chabraszewski; 249 BlueSkyImage; cartoon images courtesy of: krasivo, Sabelskaya, Rvector, Diego Schtutman, Lina Truman, I000s_pixels, LITUSPRO, Sapunkele, lineartestpilot.

ISBN 978-1-78755-727-7

Manufactured in China

1 3 5 7 9 10 8 6 4 2

CODING

for Kids
2019 EDITION

ADAM CRUTE

FLAME TREE
PUBLISHING

CONTENTS

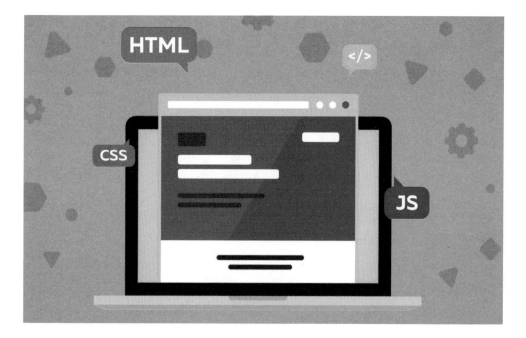

This is probably your first introduction to the languages of the internet, so we will discuss what these are, what they look like and what they do. We will cover the three languages that are most important: HTML, CSS and JavaScript. There are also four exercises in this chapter to get you started with making your first web page, using CSS to give it some style and some scripts to make things happen.

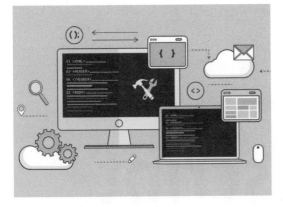

DIGGING DEEPER INTO HTML

This chapter will explain the main things you need to know about HTML5, so that using it becomes second nature after a while. It takes you through using HTML elements, with the most common ones covered, including those for headings, lists and tables. The chapter then moves on to how you can put images, video and audio on your web pages. Step-by-step guides and exercises will take you through everything involved in this and make it really simple to get to grips with.

DIGGING DEEPER INTO CSS

This chapter kicks off with how to understand CSS selectors. Among others, it covers descendant, typed class and compound selectors and how you can play around with them to improve your website's appearance. It will also take you through adding colour, element box styles, padding and margins – we will also briefly touch on sizing and positioning, which is covered in more detail in chapter 5 – to help you create the amazing design you've been imagining.

We take a look at JavaScript in this chapter, starting off with identifiers, keywords and reserved words, and then we will move on to discuss datatypes (in particular Booleans, strings and arrays). The first exercise will get you using variables – declaring them, and assigning and changing their values. The second exercise will cover objects, and the third will teach you when it is necessary to use if statements. This is only a taster of the large amount of ground we cover in this exciting chapter.

PLAYING WITH CODE

The final chapter of this book has some really great exercises to put everything you've learned into practice. Build Starfleet Defence, in which enemy spacecraft have been detected and must be destroyed! We take you through everything from how to prepare the project folder to taking your first shot. After this, we move on to Hungry Man – a word guessing game – as well as CodeBreaker, a real test of whether you can crack the hidden code.

INTRODUCTION

Programming – often referred to as coding – is fun. No, really, it is! There's tremendous satisfaction to be had when a bunch of peculiar words and symbols that you've written makes something cool happen on your computer screen.

WELCOME TO THE FUN WORLD OF CODING

This book aims to help you achieve that sense of satisfaction by taking you on a journey through the languages of the internet, heading for a final destination in which you will code three cool little computer games.

What We Will Be Covering

The subjects we're going to be looking at are relatively simple in the big, wide world

Hot Tips

The downloadable code package for this book can be downloaded from www.flametreepublishing.com/book-samples.html. Once downloaded, double-click the file to unzip it so that you can access its folders and files.

of programming. This book is not about complex coding – we'll leave that to other books. We'll be focusing on the essentials you need to know to produce your own web pages and simple games.

DOWNLOADABLE CODE PACKAGE

We've prepared a package of files that accompany the exercises and step-by-step walkthroughs in this book. The package contains starting points for all of the exercises in the book; these are especially important when we reach Chapter 5: Playing With Code (see page 198). You can download the package from our website, here: www.flametreepublishing.com/book-samples.html

Pre-built Code

Even the simplest of computer games requires some quite advanced coding techniques to be used, and the simple fact is that there's no way to take someone from being a beginner to an advanced coder in a book of this size. Therefore the games you will be coding in Chapter 5 depend on you working with the pre-built code that we have provided in the downloadable package; the games won't work without it.

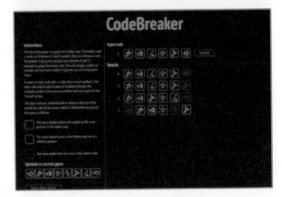

Above: This book will take you from being a beginner to coding these fun little games.

TOOLS OF THE TRADE

While web pages can be developed using nothing more than a basic text editor, much better tools are available at little to no cost. Also, most developers use graphics editing software, as well as multiple web browsers.

CODE EDITING

HTML, CSS and JavaScript are all written as plain text. This means that – at the bare minimum – all you need to code web pages is the basic text editor that's built into your operating system (Notepad on Windows; TextEdit on Mac; Vim on Linux-based systems). This works OK save for a few pitfalls, but there's a far superior solution available: IDEs.

IDEs

An IDE, or Integrated Development Environment, is a piece of software that helps you to write other pieces of software. IDEs help both with writing scripts – speeding up your work and helping you to spot errors – and with managing the many files that make up a full website or large project. The image on the page opposite shows some of the super-helpful features of IDEs.

Hot Tips

TextEdit on a Mac can create plain text and rich text files, so if using it as your code editor, be sure to switch all new files to plain text mode by selecting Make Plain Text from the 'Format' menu.

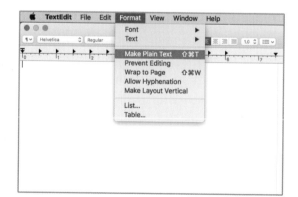

Above: HTML, CSS and JavaScript have to be written in plain text files: don't use Rich Text!

Which IDE Should I Use?

There are loads of IDEs available. Some, such as Adobe Dreamweaver (www.adobe.com) are only available under commercial licensing; others are available under open-source licence, meaning they are free to install and use. Choosing and using IDEs can be bewildering, so to save you those headaches we recommend you download and install Komodo Edit: it's free, easy to get to grips with, and is available from www.activestate.com/komodo-ide/downloads/edit.

Integrated file manager assists with managing a project's many files and folders

Tabbed editor lets you open a number of files from a project and easily flip between them

Code colouring highlights different parts of the code, making it more readable

Indent-level markers ensure you can easily match opening and closing tags

Automatic code indentation helps with legibility and makes the code's structure easier to understand

Line numbering helps you to navigate within a large document, and can help when tracking down bugs and errors

Code hints as you type speed up coding. reduce spelling mistakes, and help you to find the element/ command etc. that you're looking for

Code folding lets you hide sections of code that you aren't currently interested in (notice the jump in the line numbers)

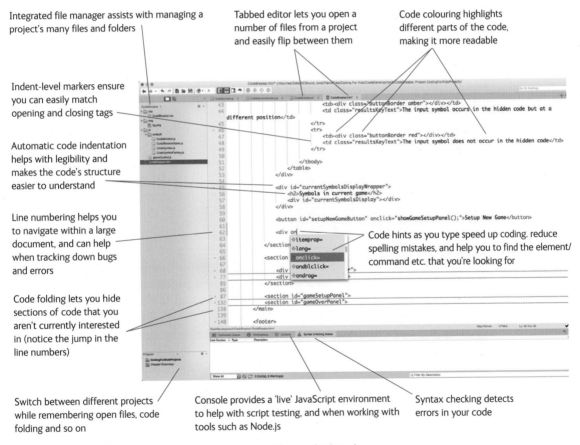

Switch between different projects while remembering open files, code folding and so on

Console provides a 'live' JavaScript environment to help with script testing, and when working with tools such as Node.js

Syntax checking detects errors in your code

Above: Komodo Edit provides many useful features to aid with developing and coding web pages.

IMAGE AND GRAPHICS EDITORS

You will often find yourself needing to edit images and create designs and graphics for your web pages and sites. The tools for these tasks are an image editor and a graphics editor. For a long time, the professional choice has been a pricey combination of Adobe Photoshop and Adobe Illustrator, and this remains a powerful pairing, but Adobe's dominance is being challenged, not least by Serif's similarly powerful but far less expensive Affinity Photo and Affinity Designer.

If you're looking for free, open-source solutions, or are working in a Linux operating system, then GIMP is your best option for image editing, and Inkscape will serve you well for creating graphics.

- Affinity Photo / Affinity Designer (Win/Mac): affinity.serif.com
- Adobe Photoshop / Adobe Illustrator (Win/Mac): www.adobe.com
- GIMP (Win/Mac/Linux): www.gimp.org
- Inkscape (Win/Mac/Linux): inkscape.org

Above: There are a range of image and graphics editors out there; which to choose is down to personal preference and budget.

Web Browsers

Web browsers sometimes handle code differently to one another, and so you may spend ages lovingly crafting a page to look and work just how you want it to, only to find that when opened in a different browser, the layout goes to pot and some of the scripts don't work. This was a much bigger problem in the past than it is now, but web developers still test their pages in as many different web browsers as possible.

All of the examples in this book use standard HTML, CSS and JavaScript programming techniques and constructs. However, in order to side-step any annoying browser compatibility issues, we'll be using the Firefox browser for running all examples, and encourage you to do the same.

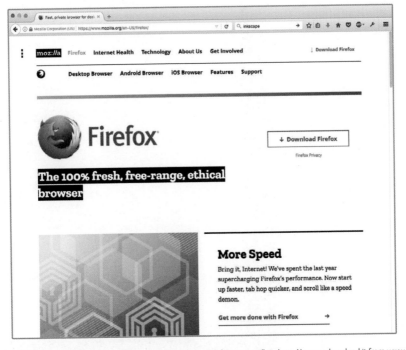

Above: Mozilla Firefox is a very 'standards-compliant' web browser, and is free to install and use. You can download it from www.mozilla.org

THE LANGUAGES OF THE INTERNET

A TERRIFIC TRIO

There are three core languages that are used to create web pages: HTML is used to describe the underlying structure and content; CSS defines the visual appearance and layout; and JavaScript controls interaction between the user and the page.

WHAT IS HTML?

HTML – or HyperText Markup Language to give it its official title – is the framework upon which all websites are built. If a website were a house, HTML would be the bricks and mortar.

```
1  <h1>HTML is a collection of elements</h1>
2  <h2>These elements start and end with a tag</h2>
3  <p>Each element has a name - it is included in the tag</p>
4  <p>Whatever appears between the opening and closing tag is the content of the element</p>
```

Above: HTML is made up of elements, which are defined by tags.

HTML is made up of **elements** – the bricks in our imaginary house – and an element starts and ends with something known as a **tag** – the mortar, if you will.

There are many different elements, most of which have a specific intended use. For example, the 'video' element is used to – can you guess? – yes, display a video. When a bunch of elements are put together in a suitable order, you have a web page.

What Does HTML Look Like?

HTML is written as plain text. To create the aforementioned video element, we would write an **opening tag**, `<video>`, and a matching **closing tag**, `</video>`. As you can see, the opening tag starts with '<', states the element name 'video', and then finishes with '>'. The closing tag follows the same pattern, but we insert a '/' before the element name. When a web browser encounters this element, it creates a video player on the screen. Simple, huh?

```
 9    <body>
10
11        <video>
12        </video>
13
14    </body>
15
```

Above: A video element does exactly what its name suggests: it creates a video player on a page.

What's Inside An Element?

So, what goes between those elements? In most circumstances, it's text and/or other elements. This means that HTML defines a structure of elements 'nested' within other elements; every element (with the exception of the special `<html>` element – *see page 30*) has a **parent** element. This is another way of naming the element that contains it. Many elements also have **child** elements – in other words the elements they contain.

Hot Tip

Code development relies heavily on the concept of 'nested' structures and 'parent/child' relationships, where one thing is defined within another.

```
22    <body onload="initialiseGame();">
23        <header>
24            <h1>CodeBreaker</h1>
25        </header>
26
27        <main>
28
29            <section id="leftPanel">
30                <div id="instructions">
31                    <h2>Instructions</h2>
32                    <p>The aim of the game is to guess the hidden code. The hidden code is made up of between 4 and 8 symbols, the
33                    <p>To enter an input code, left- or right-click on each symbol in the input code area to cycle forward or back
34                    <p>The input code you submitted will be shown at the top of the results list, and will be colour-coded to indi
35
36                    <table id="resultsKeyTable">
37                        <tbody>
38                            <tr>
39                                <td><div class="buttonBorder green"></div></td>
40                                <td class="resultsKeyText">The input symbol matches the symbol at the same position in the hidden
41                            </tr>
42                            <tr>
43                                <td><div class="buttonBorder amber"></div></td>
44                                <td class="resultsKeyText">The input symbol occurs in the hidden code but at a different position
45                            </tr>
46                            <tr>
47                                <td><div class="buttonBorder red"></div></td>
48                                <td class="resultsKeyText">The input symbol does not occur in the hidden code</td>
49                            </tr>
50
51                        </tbody>
52                    </table>
53                </div>
54
55                <div id="currentSymbolsDisplayWrapper">
56                    <h2>Symbols in current game</h2>
57                    <div id="currentSymbolsDisplay"></div>
58                </div>
59
60                <button id="setupNewGameButton" onclick="showGameSetupPanel();">Setup New Game</button>
61
62            </section>
```

Above: When writing HTML, most developers indent lines of code with the Tab key to make it easier to see the way a page's elements are nested. IDEs like Komodo Edit can manage this indentation for you.

Modifying Elements

While all HTML elements have an intended use, most can be modified in various ways too. For example, we may want to set the dimensions of a video player or image, or the font size of text.

Elements are modified by adjusting the **attributes** of the element, and this is done in the opening tag, for example:

```
<video width="1024" height="576">
```

Hot Tip

When writing attribute values, you can use single or double quote marks, but it is vital to be consistent in which you use.

As you can see, an attribute name is declared within the opening tag, followed by '=' and then a **value** wrapped inside quote marks.

```
23
24        <video width="1024" height="576" controls="1" src="vids/myVideo.mp4" />
25
```

Above: Attributes allow you to modify an element in some way.

The Components of HTML

- **Element:** The basic building block of HTML

- **Tag:** Defines the start and end of an element

- **Attribute:** Modifies an element in some useful way

GETTING STYLISH

In old versions of HTML, there were loads of different attributes for controlling the visual appearance and layout of elements. What's more, different elements had wildly varying sets of attributes that would work with them.

Remembering which attributes worked with which elements was a nightmare, and so the `style` attribute was developed.

Style Rules

The value assigned to the `style` attribute is called a **style rule** and this consists of one or more **style commands**. A style command is a pairing of a **style property** and a value to be applied to that property, for example:

```
<section style="color:green; font-weight:bold;">
```

Each style property (`color` and `font-weight` in this example) is followed by a colon (:), then the value to be assigned to that property, and finally a semicolon (;).

```
 9
▾10     <section style="color:green; font-weight: bold;">
11      |
12      </section>
13
```

Above: The style attribute allows you to control the visual appearance of an element.

WHAT IS CSS?

When we add a style rule to an element's `style` attribute it is known as **Inline** styling. It works, but it has a problem: if you want to change, say, the text color of all of your text headings, then you have to edit the `color` style property in every occurrence of a heading element. This is where CSS comes into the picture.

CSS stands for 'Cascading Style Sheets'. It allows us to define the style rules that will apply to different elements in a web page, and separates those definitions from the HTML code they apply to. A big benefit of this is that any changes made to a CSS style rule will affect all elements that are associated with that rule.

```
4  p {
5      font-size: 14px;
6      color: white;
7      text-align: center;
8      margin: 4px;
9  }
```

Above: CSS can apply the same style rule to multiple elements at the same time, for example all <p> elements would be styled by this rule.

What Does CSS Look Like?

Like HTML, CSS is plain text written with a special structure. CSS code comprises **selectors** and style rules; the selector specifies the HTML element(s) that the following style rule will be applied to. The style rule itself is wrapped in curly brackets, '{' and '}' following the selector. A collection of selectors and associated style rules is called a **style sheet**.

```
43 h2 {
44      font-size: 18px;
45      font-weight: 700;
46      margin: 0px 10px 5px 10px;
47      filter: drop-shadow(0px 0px 3px rgba(74,165,247,0.9));
48 }
```

Above: A style sheet is made up of selectors followed by style rules wrapped in curly brackets.

A Selection of Selectors

At its simplest, a selector is nothing more than the name of the HTML element that will receive the selector's style rule (this is called a **Type** selector). For example, a p selector will target all of the <p> elements in a page. There are other forms of selector, such as **ID** and **Class** selectors (not to mention ways of combining selectors) that allow you to target specific groups of elements, or even individual elements.

CASCADING STYLE SHEET (CSS)

Why 'Cascading'?

When a web browser draws – or **renders** – an HTML element, it has to work out which style rules to apply to that element. This is straightforward enough if the element in question has one – and only one – matching selector in the style sheet. But what if there's no matching selector, or more than one matching selector? How does the browser work out which style properties to apply to the element?

The first method is called **inheritance**: elements 'inherit' many of the style properties of their parent element (and their parent's parent element, and so on) if those properties are not specifically defined for an element.

Hot Tip

An element's 'parent' is the element within which it is located. When an element has other elements within it, these inner elements are known as 'children' or 'child elements' of that element.

The second method is **specificity**, and this comes into play when an element matches with more than one selector and so receives more than one style rule. When this happens, the browser works out which of the style rules is more 'specific' to a given element, and the style properties from this rule will override any matching properties from less specific rules, as well as any inherited rules.

Hot Tip

Web browsers have their own built-in default style sheet. This sits at the top of the style sheet cascade and defines basic styling for all elements. If you don't override these default rules with your own, then it is this basic styling that you'll see.

```css
 9 body {
10     font-family: 'PT Sans Narrow', sans-serif;
11     background-color: #000C20;
12     background-image: url("../img/bg.png");
13     background-repeat: repeat-x;
14     background-attachment: fixed;
15     background-position: 0px 0px;
16     color: #4AA5F7;
17     margin: 0px;
18 }
19
20 header {
21     text-align: center;
22 }
23
24     header h1 {
25         font-size: 72px;
26         font-weight: 700;
27         text-align: center;
28         margin: 0px auto 10px auto;
29         padding-top: 10px;
30         filter: drop-shadow(0px 0px 5px rgba(74,165,247,0.7));
31     }
32
33 main {
34     width: 1024px;
35     height: 768px;
36     margin: 20px auto 20px auto;
37 }
38
39 section {
40     text-align: left;
41 }
42
43 h2 {
44     font-size: 18px;
45     font-weight: 700;
46     margin: 0px 10px 5px 10px;
47     filter: drop-shadow(0px 0px 3px rgba(74,165,247,0.9));
48 }
```

Ultimately, what we end up with is a set of style properties and style rules that 'cascade' through the HTML document's structure, and to which the browser can refer to determine the correct styling to apply to any and every HTML element.

Components of CSS

○ Selector: Targets the HTML element(s) that a style rule will be applied to

○ Style command: Specifies a CSS property and assigns a value to it (aka a 'property-value pair')

○ Style rule: A collection of style properties and their associated values

Left: A section of a CSS style sheet showing multiple selectors and style rules.

WHAT IS JAVASCRIPT?

JavaScript is a **scripting language** that's used to interact with and control pages loaded into a web browser. It provides loads of tools and methods for interacting with the user, the page and the internet.

What does JavaScript look like?

Just like HTML and CSS, JavaScript is written as plain text, but it is a much more complex and fussy beast than either HTML or CSS. We'll be getting our hands dirty with a fair bit of JavaScript later in the book, but we won't be delving too deeply into the masses of detail that surrounds the language (we'll leave that to other books, such as *Coding JavaScript Basics*).

```
116 com.flametreepublishing.cfk.Spacecraft.prototype.positionSpacecraft = function(aContext, aCoordinate) {
117     if (aContext.hitTest(aCoordinate) != "miss") {
118         return(false);
119     }
120     var layoutOptions = this.getLayoutOptions(aContext, aCoordinate);
121     if (layoutOptions.length == 0) {
122         return(false);
123     }
124     var randomDirectionIndex = Math.floor(Math.random() * layoutOptions.length);
125     var layoutDirection = layoutOptions[randomDirectionIndex];
126     this.craftCoords = new Array();
127     this.craftCoords.push(aCoordinate);
128     for(var i = 1; i < this.craftSize; i++) {
129         var newCoordinate = new com.flametreepublishing.cfk.TargetingCoordinate();
130         if (layoutDirection == "north") {
131             newCoordinate.setCoordinates(aCoordinate.x, aCoordinate.y -i);
132         } else if (layoutDirection == "east") {
133             newCoordinate.setCoordinates(aCoordinate.x + i, aCoordinate.y);
134         } else if (layoutDirection == "south") {
135             newCoordinate.setCoordinates(aCoordinate.x, aCoordinate.y +i);
136         } else if (layoutDirection == "west") {
137             newCoordinate.setCoordinates(aCoordinate.x -i, aCoordinate.y);
138         }
139         this.craftCoords.push(newCoordinate);
140     }
141     return(true);
142 }
```

Above: JavaScript can get quite complicated, but it is often not as complicated as it appears.

What is a Script?

In the world of the theatre, a script can be thought of as a series of instructions that tell the actors in a production where to be, what to do and say, and when to do and say it. In computing, the meaning is very similar: a script is a series of instructions for the computer to perform. Yes, the actors are onscreen graphics and chunks of data rather than a troupe of thespians, but the principle remains the same.

JavaScript Runs on the 'Client Side'

It's important to understand from the outset that when using JavaScript on a web page, it runs on the user's – or client's – computer, and interacts with the web page that's loaded on to the web browser on that computer. This arrangement is referred to as 'client-side' scripting.

Above: A script tells the actors where to be, what to do, and when to do it... the actors being computer data and graphics, of course!

JavaScript is not Java

You may have heard of a language called Java and think it relates in some way to JavaScript – it doesn't! Java was a hot topic at the time JavaScript was developed and by naming the language JavaScript its developers ensured that it got noticed. Other than a passing similarity in some parts of their **syntax** though, the two languages are fundamentally different and unrelated.

Hot Tip

The word 'syntax' often crops up in coding, and refers to the allowed structure of any code that's written in a given language.

Why Include Scripts in a Page?

There are almost as many reasons for using scripting on a page as there are pages that use scripting! In general though, there are two key reasons for using scripts: to modify the appearance of a page, and/or to allow communication between a page and a web server – this book is only concerned with the first of these reasons.

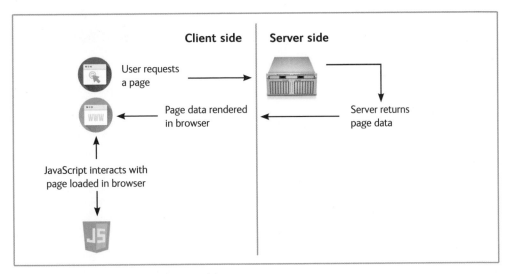

Above: JavaScript interacts with the user, the page and the internet.

EXERCISE 1:
YOUR FIRST WEB PAGE

The best way to learn coding is to dive in and get your hands dirty with some code, so let's do just that by creating your first web page.

CREATE A WORKING FOLDER

The first thing to do is create a folder in which to store all of the files for your page. Your Documents folder would be a good place for this; better still, create a folder called MySites inside your Home folder, and use this as a central location for all of the pages and sites you develop. Wherever you put it, the folder you create for an individual site should have the same name as the site – let's call this one MyFirstWebPage.

Right: Always create a new outer folder for any new coding project.

	MySites			
Name	^	Date Modified	Size	Kind
▼ 📁 MyFirstWebPage		Today, 13:56	--	Folder

1 item, 515.1 GB available

CREATE THE HTML FILE AND BASIC STRUCTURAL ELEMENTS

1. In your code editor or IDE, create a new file and save it as MyFirstWebPage.htm. The **file extension** – that's the end bit of the filename following the fullstop – for an HTML file should always be '.htm' or '.html'.

2. At the very top of the new HTML document, enter the following code:

```
<!DOCTYPE HTML>
```

This special tag – called the **DocType Declaration** – tells the web browser that what follows will be HTML5 (see page 64). This tag must appear at the top of all of your HTML5 documents, and does not require a matching closing tag.

3. Tap the enter key a couple of times and then type the following opening tag:

```
<html>
```

If you're using an IDE, the closing tag, `</html>`, will probably be added for you; if not, then add this closing tag on the next line down.

Hot Tip

Don't use spaces when naming files or folders. Either remove the spaces and capitalize each word (known as 'CamelCase'), or replace the spaces with underscores (My_First_Web_Page.htm).

```
1  <!DOCTYPE HTML>
2
3  <html>
4  </html>
```

Above: All HTML documents must contain a Doc Type Declaration and a single `<html>` element.

The <html> Element

Every HTML document must contain one, and only one, <html> element. Every other element in the document must be nested, or contained, within this single <html> element.

Thinking about our earlier discussion on HTML's nested structure (*see* page 18), the <html> element is the beginning of that structure. Because of this it is often referred to as the **root** of the document.

The <html> element itself always contains two, and only two, child elements: the <head> element and the <body> element. Let's add those to the page now.

ADDING THE <HEAD> AND <BODY> ELEMENTS

1. Create a couple of empty lines inside the `<html>` element. When loading a document, web browsers ignore empty lines, spaces and tab indents – known as **whitespace** – and this allows us to space out and indent our HTML code to make it easier to read.

2. If you aren't using an IDE, which will control code indenting automatically, hit the tab key on your keyboard to create an indent. Add a `<head>` opening tag, an empty line, and then the matching closing tag `</head>`.

3. Add another empty line and then add the `<body>` element (don't forget to add the closing tag!).

```
1  <!DOCTYPE HTML>
2
3  <html>
4
5      <head>
6
7      </head>
8
9      <body>
10
11     </body>
12
13 </html>
```

Above: When creating a new HTML file, always add this structure before doing anything else.

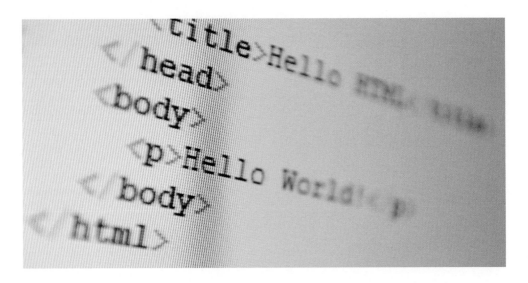

4. The `<head>` of the document is where we place elements that provide information about the page, style rules, and links to other files that the page needs; one thing that we commonly define in the `<head>` is the title that will appear at the top of the web browser. Add the following within the `<head>`:

```
<title>My First Web
Page</title>
```

5. `<meta>` elements are used for providing additional information to the browser; the information itself is defined by the element's attribute and attribute value. We need to tell the page what **character set** to use (see Hot Tip, above), so add the following to the page's `<head>`:

```
<meta
charset="utf-8" />
```

```
 5      <head>
 6          <title>My First Web Page</title>
 7      </head>
 8
 9      <body>
10
11      </body>
```

Above: The text inside the `<title>` element is displayed at the top of the browser window or tab.

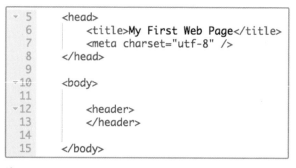

Hot Tip

Inside a computer, all data, including text, is represented by numbers. A character set, then, is a table that maps those numbers to text characters; typically, you will use `utf-8` for all of your pages.

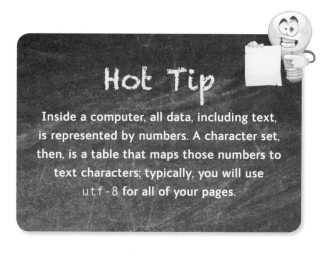

```
 5      <head>
 6          <title>My First Web Page</title>
 7          <meta charset="utf-8" />
 8      </head>
 9
10      <body>
11
12          <header>
13          </header>
14
15      </body>
```

Above: `<meta>` elements provide information to the browser, and are written as self-closing tags.

Self-closing Tags

You may have noticed that the `<meta>` element you have just added does not have a matching closing tag, but instead its opening tag ends with `/ >`. This is known as a **self-closing tag**, and the reason it is self-closing is because it cannot contain child elements. Strictly speaking, in HTML5 we don't need to include the `/` before the `>`, but many developers consider it a 'best practice' nonetheless. We will encounter more self-closing tags soon.

THE <BODY> ELEMENT

The `<body>` element is, as the name suggests, the main content area of the page; it is where we place all of the elements that will create a visual output on the screen. Typically, we split the `<body>` into three sections: a header, a main area, and a footer. Let's do that now.

STRUCTURING THE <BODY> ELEMENT

1. Most pages have an area at the top in which to display a logo, page title, navigation menu and so on – in HTML we refer to this as the 'header' (not to be confused with the document's `<head>` element). To create the header section, add the following inside the page's body:

   `<header>`

   Don't forget to add a closing tag if your IDE doesn't do so automatically.

2. The main area of the page is where we place all of the important content - the stuff that the page is all about. Add the following below the header:

   `<main>`

   Again, don't forget the closing tag.

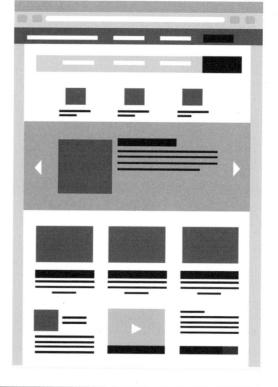

```
 ▾ 5      <head>
   6          <title>My First Web Page</title>
   7          <meta charset="utf-8" />
   8      </head>
   9
 ▾10      <body>
  11
 ▾12          <header>
  13          </header>
  14
  15      </body>
```

Above: Don't confuse the `<header>` with the page's `<head>` element.

3. Many pages include a footer that contains additional information about a website: contact details, useful links, copyright information and so on. Add a footer section with the `<footer>` element; as ever, don't forget the closing tag.

```
10    <body>
11
12        <header>
13        </header>
14
15        <main>
16        </main>
17
18        <footer>
19        </footer>
20
21    </body>
```

Above: Typically, we split the body into three sections; the element names for these sections are easy to remember.

HEADING TEXT

Most web pages contain text – often quite a lot of it – and so unsurprisingly, there is a collection of elements that are dedicated to displaying text. One set of those text elements is dedicated to displaying headings: their names are very easy to remember: the first is called `<h1>`, the second `<h2>` and so on until we reach `<h6>`.

Hot Tip

`<h4>` to `<h6>` are rarely used: just how many levels of heading do you need?

Heading level 1
Heading level 2
Heading level 3
Heading level 4
Heading level 5
Heading level 6

Above: There are six levels of heading element in HTML.

ADDING HEADING TEXT

1. Now we're ready to start adding some text to the page, you will need to decide what the page is to be about. You could make it about yourself, a favourite pet or toy, a hobby: it's up to you.

2. Locate the `<header>` element of your page, create a new line within it and add an `<hgroup>` element. This element is used for grouping heading elements together; we'll talk about why we do this on page 71.

3. Within the `<hgroup>`, add an `<h1>` element and type a title for your page within it.

4. Add an `<h2>` element below the `<h1>` and add a subtitle or strapline within it.

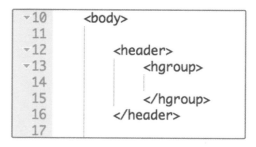

```
▼10          <body>
 11
▼12              <header>
▼13                  <hgroup>
 14
 15                  </hgroup>
 16              </header>
 17
```

Above: Create an `<hgroup>` element within the `<header>`.

```
▼12              <header>
▼13                  <hgroup>
 14                      <h1>SpiderPenguin</h1>
 15                      <h2>The world's first fish-powered superhero</h2>
 16                  </hgroup>
 17              </header>
```

Above: The page's `<header>` element is a good place to add a heading and subheading for your page.

PARAGRAPHS

Whilst there are multiple elements for displaying heading text, there is only one for paragraph, or body, text: `<p>`. In most circumstances, if we want to display non-heading text on the screen, we do so with one or more `<p>` elements.

MORE STRUCTURAL ELEMENTS

We've already met the `<header>`, `<main>` and `<footer>` elements: these are often referred to as structural elements because they create a logical structure on the web page. However, a page should only feature one occurrence of each, and they should only occur as children of the `<body>` element. Reusable structural elements exist in the form of `<section>`, `<article>`, `<aside>`, and others.

CREATING CONTENT STRUCTURE

A `<section>` element is the next structural step from `<main>`. In other words, it's intended to be used as a child of the `<main>` element. We're going to make two sections: an About section and a Blog section.

1. Locate the `<main>` element and then add within it a new `<section>` element.

2. Inside the new `<section>`, add an `<h2>` element with the text 'About' within it.

3. Add some paragraphs of text inside the `<section>`, underneath the `<h2>`. Each paragraph should be contained in its own `<p>` element; add at least two paragraphs.

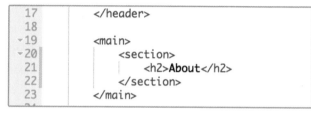

```
17        </header>
18
19        <main>
20            <section>
21                <h2>About</h2>
22            </section>
23        </main>
```

Above: Create a new section and a heading within that section.

```
20        <section>
21            <h2>About</h2>
22                <p>Following an accident involving kelp, toxic waste, a nuclear submarine and a tasty tuna fish, mild-mannered
    Peter Penguin was transformed into the one and only SpiderPenguin - the world's first fish-powered superhero. Orcas quake and
    leopard seals quiver when this penguin's goes for a swim.</p>
23                <p>SpiderPenguin's powers include casting webs, climbing walls, and catching fish in the special spider-nets he
    fires from his super-flippers.</p>
24                <p>Faster than a torpedo, stronger than a whale, and cooler than a cucumber, SpiderPenguin always saves the day</p>
25        </section>
```

Above: Add some paragraphs of text to the About section.

4. Now create the Blog section by adding a new `<section>` element below the About section. Add an `<h2>` heading with the word Blog inside it.

5. Blogs are often made up of a series of individual articles; what better way to make use of the `<article>` element? Add one within the Blog section.

```
25              </section>
26
27          <section>
28              <h2>Blog</h2>
29          </section>
30
31      </main>
32
```

Above: Add a `<section>` element with a heading of Blog.

6. Add an `<h3>` heading within the new `<article>`, and type an article title within it.

7. Add some text paragraphs to the article using `<p>` elements.

8. Repeat steps 5–7 to add one or two more articles to the Blog section, and then save your work.

```
27          <section>
28              <h2>Blog</h2>
29              <article>
30                  <h3>Rockhopper says 'Thanks SpiderPenguin!'</h3>
31                  <p>A rockhopper had cause to say a big thank you to SpiderPenguin today: Whilst resting peacefully on a
   comfy iceberg, he was spotted by a pod of orcas who proceeded to take it in turns to try to wash him off the 'berg.</p>
32                  <p>'All seemed lost' said Rocky, but then in a flash of red and blue, and a flurry of sticky web-like
   material, SpiderPenguin swooped in and plucked Rocky to safety. Phew-ee!</p>
33              </article>
34          </section>
```

Above: Add an article and give it a heading and some paragraphs of text.

OPENING YOUR PAGE

You've done quite a bit of coding now, but haven't seen the results of that hard work, so let's take a look now. In most circumstances, if you double-click an HTML file stored on your computer, it will be opened in your default web browser, and this is one way to test your file. If, however, you wish to open the file in a browser other than your default browser, then right-click on the HTML file and from the Open with (or similar, depending on OS) menu, select the browser you want to test with. Go ahead and open your first page now to see what it looks like...

... OK, so the words look good, but everything else looks a bit, well, plain. We'll tackle that in a moment.

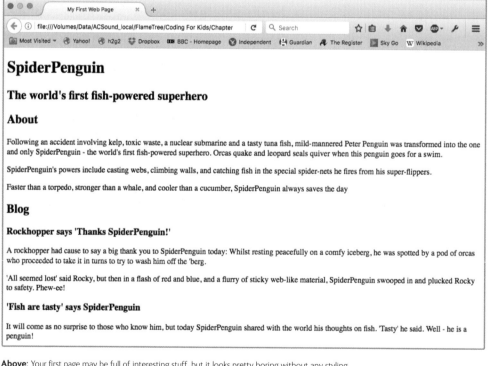

Above: Your first page may be full of interesting stuff, but it looks pretty boring without any styling.

Online Pages

Normally when opening web pages, we're doing so online. The pages you're opening aren't stored on your computer, but are located somewhere on the internet. That 'somewhere' is a web server, and in simple terms, it is little different to a folder on your computer: the web server stores files, and those files are loaded into your browser when it requests them from the server.

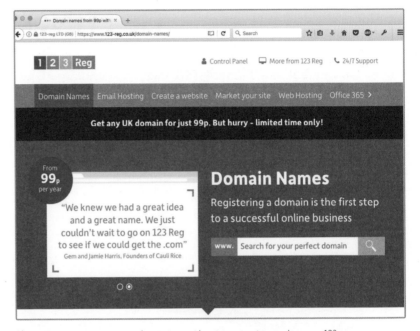

Above: You can register your own domain name with an internet registrar such as www.123-reg. co.uk. It needn't be expensive.

Getting your pages online is quite simple and needn't cost a huge amount, around £20 per year if you want your own domain name and dedicated server space. We're not going to say more about this in this book, but there are plenty of guides and how-to's online.

Hot Tip

A website's domain name is the bit of the site address that follows the 'www.'. For example, Flame Tree Publishing's domain name is flametreepublishing.com.

EXERCISE 2: GETTING STYLISH

We've created a simple HTML page, but visually it's very plain and boring. CSS is the tool to sort this out, so let's write some style rules.

EMBEDDED STYLE SHEETS

We've already mentioned inline styling, in which a `style` attribute is used to apply a style rule to an individual element. There are times when this is useful, but in general, it is better to separate the page's content, the HTML, from the page's style rules. An **embedded** style sheet is one way of doing this: the selectors and style rules are written within a `<style>` element contained in the page's `<head>` element.

EMBEDDING A STYLE SHEET AND ADDING A STYLE RULE

1. Open your MyFirstWebPage.htm file in your code editor or IDE. Locate the `<head>` element, create an empty line or two and then add a `<style>` element inside the `<head>`.

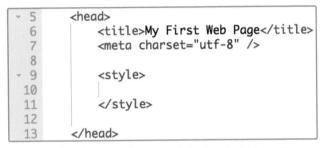

```
 5        <head>
 6            <title>My First Web Page</title>
 7            <meta charset="utf-8" />
 8
 9            <style>
10
11            </style>
12
13        </head>
```

Above: `<style>` elements are always written in the `<head>` of a document.

2. Within the `<style>` element, type the word body followed by an opening curly bracket {, two carriage returns and a closing curly bracket }. What you have done is create a body selector – the style rule we'll write inside the curly brackets will be applied to the `<body>` element, and will cascade through the document unless overridden by another rule.

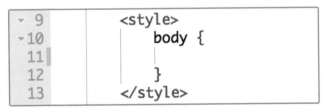

```
 9            <style>
10                body {
11
12                }
13            </style>
```

Above: The style rule written between the curly brackets will be applied to the `<body>` element.

3. Because the `body` selector's style rule will cascade through the document, it is a good place to set some default style properties, such as the main font to use. Add the following code inside the `body` selector's curly brackets:

```
font-family: "Arial", sans-serif;
```

```
 9      <style>
10          body {
11              font-family: "Arial", sans-serif;
12          }
13
14      </style>
```

Above: The `body` selector targets the `<body>` HTML element.

4. Save your page and then open it in your web browser. It's still fairly ugly, but notice that the font has changed throughout the document: headings are still bolder and larger than paragraphs, but the font itself is the same throughout; the style property has cascaded through the document from the `<body>` element.

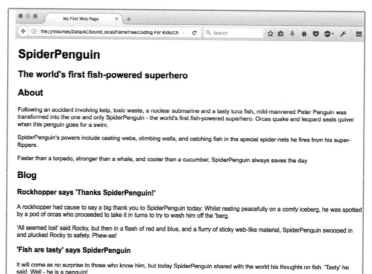

Right: The `font-family` style property set on the `<body>` element cascades through the entire page.

FONTS IN WEB PAGES

Until quite recently, web developers had a bit of a problem when it came to fonts, and that problem was that a web page could only use a font that was already installed on the end user's computer, so developers could only use fonts that were common across all computers... that's not a big list of fonts!

CSS font-family style property

In CSS, we select fonts using the `font-family` style property. This style property takes as its value a list of font names separated by commas; the font names are enclosed in quote marks. A browser will look to see if it has the first font in the list; if it does, this font will be used; if not, then the browser will look to the next font in the list, and so on.

Hot Tip

In the world of typography, a serif is a little tick or embellishment added to letters, so a serif font is one that has such embellishments, such as Times New Roman. A sans-serif font does not have such embellishments: Arial and Helvetica are well-known sans-serif fonts.

Serif

Serif fonts have embellishments on the letters

Sans-serif

San-serif fonts have no embellishments on the letters

Above: Serif fonts have serifs; sans-serif fonts do not.

CSS Default Fonts

The last item in a font-family value is normally either serif or sans-serif (and, unlike the other font names, we don't enclose this font name in quote marks). These, and a few others, are default, fall-back fonts that the browser can use if it can't find any of the other fonts specified, and you should always include a default font in your own font-family values.

Web Fonts

The situation with fonts is much improved these days thanks to something called web fonts. These are fonts that a web browser can download when needed, meaning you can be sure the person viewing your page is seeing what you intend them to see; we'll learn how to use web fonts in later exercises.

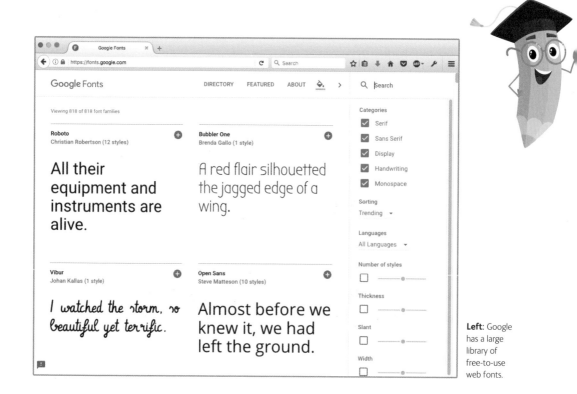

Left: Google has a large library of free-to-use web fonts.

FONT SIZE

You're probably used to setting font size as a point size, but in CSS, we use different measurement units - when talking font size, that's typically pixels or ems. Pixels are, in effect, equivalent to the point sizing you are familiar with, whilst ems are a measurement based on the size of a font's 'm' character; we'll be sticking with pixel sizing in this book.

FONT WEIGHT

Most fonts have different thicknesses available: light, regular, bold, etc. In CSS, we specify this thickness with the `font-weight` style property. The value of this property is a number between 100 and 900. Typically, 400 equates to regular weight, 300 to a light or thin weight and 700 is bold.

STYLING THE HEADINGS

1. We're using three levels of heading – <h1> to <h3>. At the moment, they're using the same font as the rest of the page – we're going to change that to Verdana. Also, we'll tweak the font sizes and weights to get a pleasing balance between the three heading levels.

2. We can link CSS selectors together in various ways: one method is to list a number of selectors separated by commas. This will result in the style rule being applied to any elements that match any item in the selector list. Within the <style> element, add the following code:

```
h1, h2, h3 {
   font-family: "Verdana",
sans-serif;
   font-weight: 700;
}
```

Hot Tip

As you will see, there are various ways to combine CSS selectors, and each separates the selectors in different ways: be sure to use the correct separator, otherwise you won't get the result you intended.

```
 9      <style>
10          body {
11              font-family: "Arial", sans-serif;
12          }
13
14          h1, h2, h3 {
15              font-family: "Verdana", sans-serif;
16              font-weight: 700;
17          }
18
19      </style>
```

Above: Multiple selectors allow us to target one style rule at a number of different elements.

3. CSS allows us to use the same selector(s) multiple times in a style sheet, so we can add individual selectors for each heading level, despite having already targeted those headings with a previous style rule. Add the following code to your style sheet:

```
h1 {
    font-size: 36px;
}
```

```
18
19      h1 {
20          font-size: 36px;
21      }
22
```

Above: Set the font size for `<h1>` elements.

Note that because we aren't setting the font-family style property in this rule, our previous rule will still apply to `<h1>` elements. Also note that the `font-size` value is followed by 'px' - this informs the browser that the measurement is given in pixels.

4. Add an h2 selector and set the `font-size` to 18px, and an h3 selector with `font-size` set to 14px.

```
9   <style>
10      body {
11          font-family: "Arial", sans-serif;
12      }
13
14      h1, h2, h3 {
15          font-family: "Verdana", sans-serif;
16          font-weight: 700;
17      }
18
19      h1 {
20          font-size: 36px;
21      }
22
23      h2 {
24          font-size: 18px;
25      }
26
27      h3 {
28          font-size: 14px;
29      }
30
31  </style>
```

Left: Your style sheet should now be looking something like this.

5. Save your work and open the page in your browser. It's starting to look better: headings are distinct from paragraphs, and the different levels of heading are obvious. One problem, however, is the look of the <h2> element that displays the subtitle/strapline in the <header>: it's the same size as subsequent <h2> elements and so doesn't look quite right, so let's change it.

6. CSS selectors can target an element based on where it is in the structure of the document. One method is to use a **descendant** selector, where we list multiple selectors separated by spaces. Add the following to your style sheet:

```
header h2 {
    font-weight: 400;
}
```

```
30
31
32
33
34
```

```
header h2 {
    font-weight: 400;
}
```

Above: Descendant selectors list two or more selectors separated by spaces.

7. What this new selector means is 'select all <h2> elements that are nested at any level within a <header> element'. This selector has a higher specificity (see page 23) than the other h2 selectors, and so overrides any matching style properties from those selectors.

8. Save your work and open the page. OK, things are still quite plain and boring, but the fonts are looking nicer and the headings have a nice hierarchy in their sizes. There's a lot more to do: colours, indents and so on, and so we'll continue to build on and improve the page over the next few exercises.

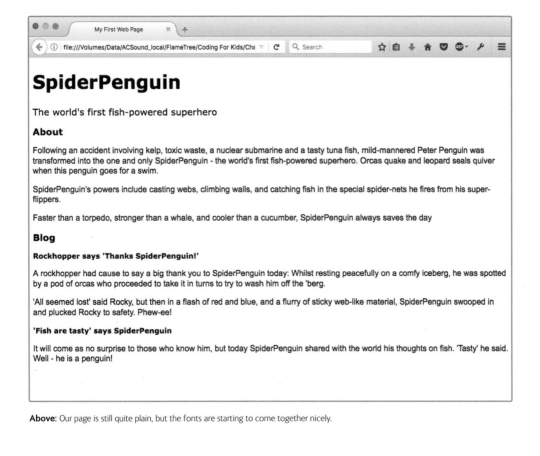

Above: Our page is still quite plain, but the fonts are starting to come together nicely.

EXERCISE 3:
MAKING THINGS HAPPEN

HTML allows us to create a structure for a page as well as allowing us to write the actual page content; CSS allows us to change the appearance of the content; but JavaScript is where we turn if we want to make things happen during or after the page loads into a browser.

ADDING A SCRIPT TO A PAGE

We add scripts to a page by using the `<script>` element. The opening tag should always include a `type` attribute with a value of "`text/javascript`". The element should always be closed with a closing tag, `</script>`.

```
 9
10   <script type="text/javascript">
11       //JavaScript is written here
12   </script>
13
14
```

Above: Embedded JavaScript is written inside a `<script>` element.

Embedded JavaScript

To embed a script in a page, we simply write the JavaScript code within a `<script type="text/javascript">` element, which can be included anywhere in the `<head>` or `<body>` of the page.

WHAT HAPPENS WHEN A BROWSER ENCOUNTERS A SCRIPT?

When a web browser loads a page, it deals with each HTML element in turn as it works through the page. When it encounters a `<script type="text/javascript">` element, the contents of the script are passed immediately to the browser's JavaScript **interpreter** (known as

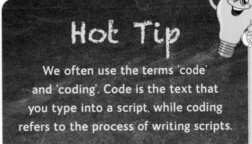

Hot Tip

We often use the terms 'code' and 'coding'. Code is the text that you type into a script, while coding refers to the process of writing scripts.

'executing' the script). It is the interpreter's job to make sense of the script and instruct the browser how to act accordingly. When the interpreter has finished executing the script, control is returned to the browser, which then continues to process and render the page.

Let's do a quick bit of coding to see this in action.

```
1  <!DOCTYPE HTML>
2  <html>
3      <head>
4          <title>A Simple Quiz</title>
5
6          <script type="text/javascript" src="js/QuizQuestion.js"></script>
7          <script type="text/javascript" src="js/SimpleQuiz.js"></script>
8          <script type="text/javascript" src="js/quizStartup.js"></script>
9
10     </head>
11
12     <body>|
13
14
15     </body>
16 </html>
17
```

```
1  //Declare a namespace
2  var com;
3  if(!com) {
4      com = {};
5  }
6  if(!com.flametreepublishing) {
7      com.flametreepublishing = {};
8  }
9
10 //Define the constructor function - this we'll
11 //place in our namespace so as not to pollute
12 //the global namespace
13 com.flametreepublishing.QuizQuestion = function(aQuestionNum, aQuestionText, aAnswers, aCorrectAnswerIndex) {
14     //The initial parameters for the question have been provided to the constructor
15     //We store them in the instance using the 'this' keyword
16     this.questionNum = aQuestionNum;
17     this.questionText = aQuestionText;
18     this.answers = aAnswers;
19     this.correctAnswerIndex = aCorrectAnswerIndex;
20 }
21
22 com.flametreepublishing.QuizQuestion.prototype.checkUserAnswer = function(answerIndex) {
23     //Create a variable to store the result of the method
24     var theResult;
25     //compare the answerIndex value to this.correctAnswerIndex
26     if(answerIndex == this.correctAnswerIndex) {
27         theResult = true;
28     } else {
```

Above: JavaScript is processed in-place as the page loads.

```
71          </main>
72
73          <footer>
74          </footer>
75
76          <script type="text/javascript">
77          </script>
78
79      </body>
80
81 </html>
```

Above: Create a `<script>` element after the `<footer>`

ADDING A SCRIPT

1. Open MyFirstWebPage.htm in your code editor or IDE. Scroll down the page and then below the `<footer>` element, add the following code:

```
<script type="text/javascript">
</script>
```

2. Anything we write inside this new `<script>` element must be written in the JavaScript language: this is very different to HTML and a lot more fiddly and complex, so we'll approach it one example at a time. Add the following inside the `<script>` element:

```
window.alert("Hi! Thanks for visiting my page");
```

3. Save the page and open it in your browser.

Hot Tip

A line of JavaScript is called a statement. Statements should always finish with a semi-colon: ;

```
75
76          <script type="text/javascript">
77              window.alert("Hi! Thanks for visiting my page");
78          </script>
79
```

Above: Add this simple script inside the `<script>` element.

HOW THE SCRIPT WORKS

The `window.alert()` command told the browser window to open a popup message panel, and the text of the message was the text contained inside the brackets; this was a block of text, or **string**, and so had to be wrapped in quote marks.

When the script was executed, the browser paused the processing of the page: you can see as much if you look at the loading animation at the top of the browser window, which will continue to spin until you clear the message by clicking the OK button. When you do this, control is returned to the browser, which proceeds to load and render the page.

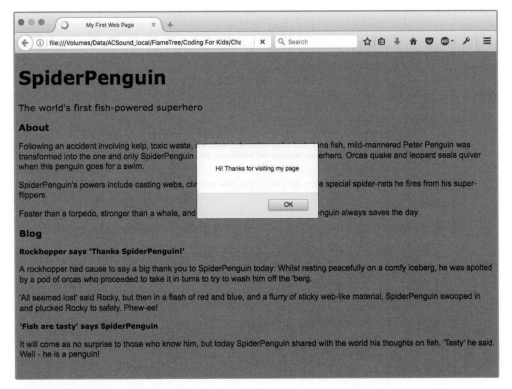

Above: The `window.alert()` command instructs the browser to display a message in a popup panel.

EXERCISE 4:
A PLACE FOR EVERYTHING

So far, we have embedded style sheets and scripts into a page. This works, but means those things are tied to the one page: what if we wanted to use the same style sheets or scripts across multiple pages, as we would for a full website?

EXTERNAL STYLE SHEETS

With an **external** style sheet, the CSS code is written in a separate document and then linked to any HTML documents you wish to apply the style sheet to. A CSS document is simply a plain text file, typically saved with a .css file extension.

Linking CSS Documents to HTML Documents

An external style sheet is associated with an HTML page using a `<link>` element placed in the `<head>` of the page:

```
<link type="text/css" rel="stylesheet" href="myCssDocument
.css" />
```

```
5    <head>
6
7        <link type="text/css" rel="stylesheet" href="myCSSDocument.css" />
8
9    </head>
```

Above: External style sheets are linked to a web page using a `<link>` element.

Link element attributes

The `<link>` element has a number of attributes that we need to set: the `type` and `rel` attributes inform the browser what type of data to expect within the targeted CSS document – always use the settings we've just shown you. The `href` attribute defines the location and name of the CSS document itself. Typically, this will be located on the same server as the web page, but often within a subfolder alongside the main HTML document.

Multiple Style Sheets

You can mix and match inline style rules with embedded and external style sheets, and an HTML document can handle as many different style rules and sheets as you wish to use. This allows you to arrange your selectors and style rules in logical groupings, with each group saved in a different CSS or HTML file. You then only need link a page to the style sheets that it needs.

```html
 3 <html>
 4
 5     <head>
 6
 7         <!-- An external style sheet -->
 8         <link type="text/css" rel="stylesheet" href="myCSSDocument.css" />
 9
10         <!-- An embedded style sheet -->
11         <style>
12             body {
13                 font-family: "Arial", sans-serif;
14                 font-size: 14px;
15                 color: white;
16                 background-color: black;
17             }
18         </style>
19
20     </head>
21
22     <body>
23
24         <!-- An inline style rule -->
25         <h1 style="font-family: 'Impact', sans-serif; font-weight: 700;">What's This All About?</h1>
26
27     </body>
28
29 </html>
```

Above: The three methods of applying CSS style rules to HTML elements.

EXTERNAL SCRIPTS

It is common to write JavaScript in a separate text file, saved with a .js file extension, and to then link this script file to any pages that need its functionality. We do this by adding the `src` attribute to a `<script>` element's opening tag. For example:

```
<script type="text/javascript" src="myScript.js"></script>
```

URLS

URL stands for Uniform Resource Locator. There are two common forms of URL: **absolute** URLs define a full address for a resource, typically starting with http://; **relative** URLs operate relative to the current file, and can only address resources within the same site as that file. A relative URL states the path from the current page to a resource, along with the resource's filename, and looks like `subfolder/name/or/names/filename.type`.

Hot Tip

When using a `<script>` element to link to an external script, we still have to include the element's closing tag `</script>`.

CREATING AN EXTERNAL STYLE SHEET AND SCRIPT

Now we know about linking to style sheets and scripts, let's update MyFirstWebPage.htm so its style sheet and script are external.

1. Use your file browser to go to the folder that contains MyFirstWebPage.htm and then create two new subfolders alongside it. Call these css and js.

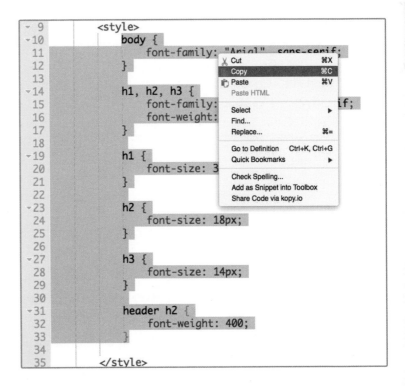

Above: It is common to put css and js subfolders alongside a page's HTML file.

2. Switch to your code editor / IDE, create a new file and save it as MyFirstCSSDoc.css within the css folder you just created.

3. Open MyFirstWebPage. htm in your editor, locate the `<style>` element, and copy its *content* – the selectors and style rules – to the clipboard ([ctrl]+[c] / [cmd]+[c]).

Rght: Copy all of the selectors and style rules from the HTML document.

```
 9    <style>
10        body {
11            font-family: "Arial", sans-serif;
12        }
13
14        h1, h2, h3 {
15            font-family:            if;
16            font-weight:
17        }
18
19        h1 {
20            font-size: 3
21        }
22
23        h2 {
24            font-size: 18px;
25        }
26
27        h3 {
28            font-size: 14px;
29        }
30
31        header h2 {
32            font-weight: 400;
33        }
34
35    </style>
```

Context menu:
- Cut ⌘X
- Copy ⌘C
- Paste ⌘V
- Paste HTML
- Select ▶
- Find...
- Replace... ⌘=
- Go to Definition Ctrl+K, Ctrl+G
- Quick Bookmarks ▶
- Check Spelling...
- Add as Snippet into Toolbox
- Share Code via kopy.io

4. Switch to your new CSS document and then paste ([ctrl]+[v] / [cmd]+[v]) the selectors and style rules into it. You may have to fiddle around a bit to remove the indenting; if you're using an IDE, then you can select the out-of-place text and press [shift]+[TAB] to reduce the indentation. Save the CSS file.

```
MyFirstCSSDoc.css  ×
 1 body {
 2     font-family: "Arial", sans-serif;
 3 }
 4
 5 h1, h2, h3 {
 6     font-family: "Verdana", sans-serif;
 7     font-weight: 700;
 8 }
 9
10 h1 {
11     font-size: 36px;
12 }
13
14 h2 {
15     font-size: 18px;
16 }
17
18 h3 {
19     font-size: 14px;
20 }
21
22 header h2 {
23     font-weight: 400;
24 }
```

Above: The style rules are now defined in an external style sheet.

5. Flip back across to the HTML file and delete the `<style>` element and all of its contents. In its place, add the following code:

```
<link type="text/css" rel="stylesheet" href="css/
MyFirstCSSDoc.css" />
```

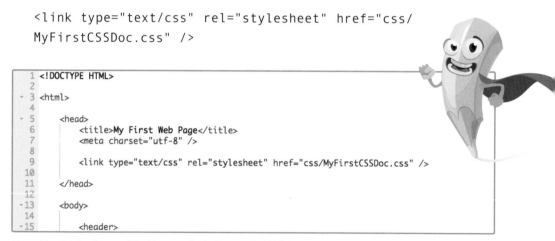

```
 1 <!DOCTYPE HTML>
 2
 3 <html>
 4
 5     <head>
 6         <title>My First Web Page</title>
 7         <meta charset="utf-8" />
 8
 9         <link type="text/css" rel="stylesheet" href="css/MyFirstCSSDoc.css" />
10
11     </head>
12
13     <body>
14
15         <header>
```

Above: The `<link>` element will load the external style sheet into the HTML document.

6. Scroll down to the `<script>` element, and then select and cut its contents ([ctrl]+[x] / [cmd]+[x]).

7. Create a new file and save it as MyFirstJS.js within the js folder you created in step 1.

Above: Save the JavaScript file inside the js folder.

8. Paste ([ctrl]+[v] / [cmd]+[v]) the code you just cut from the HTML file into the new JavaScript file, and remove any indentation if it has also copied across. Save the file.

9. Finally, flip back over to the HTML file, locate the `<script>` element, and in its opening tag add a `src` attribute with a value of `"js/MyFirstJS.js"`. You can also remove the now-unused whitespace from inside the `<script>` element. What you're left with should look like this:

```
<script type="text/javascript" src="js/MyFirstJS.js"></script>
```

```
-47          <footer>
48          </footer>
49
50          <script type="text/javascript" src="js/MyFirstJS.js"></script>
51
52      </body>
53
54 </html>
```

Above: The <script> element links the page to the external JavaScript file.

10. Save your work and then open the web page in your browser. All being well, everything should be exactly as it was before, but now the style sheet and script are being pulled in from separate files.

Right: The page looks the same, but it's now linked to external resources.

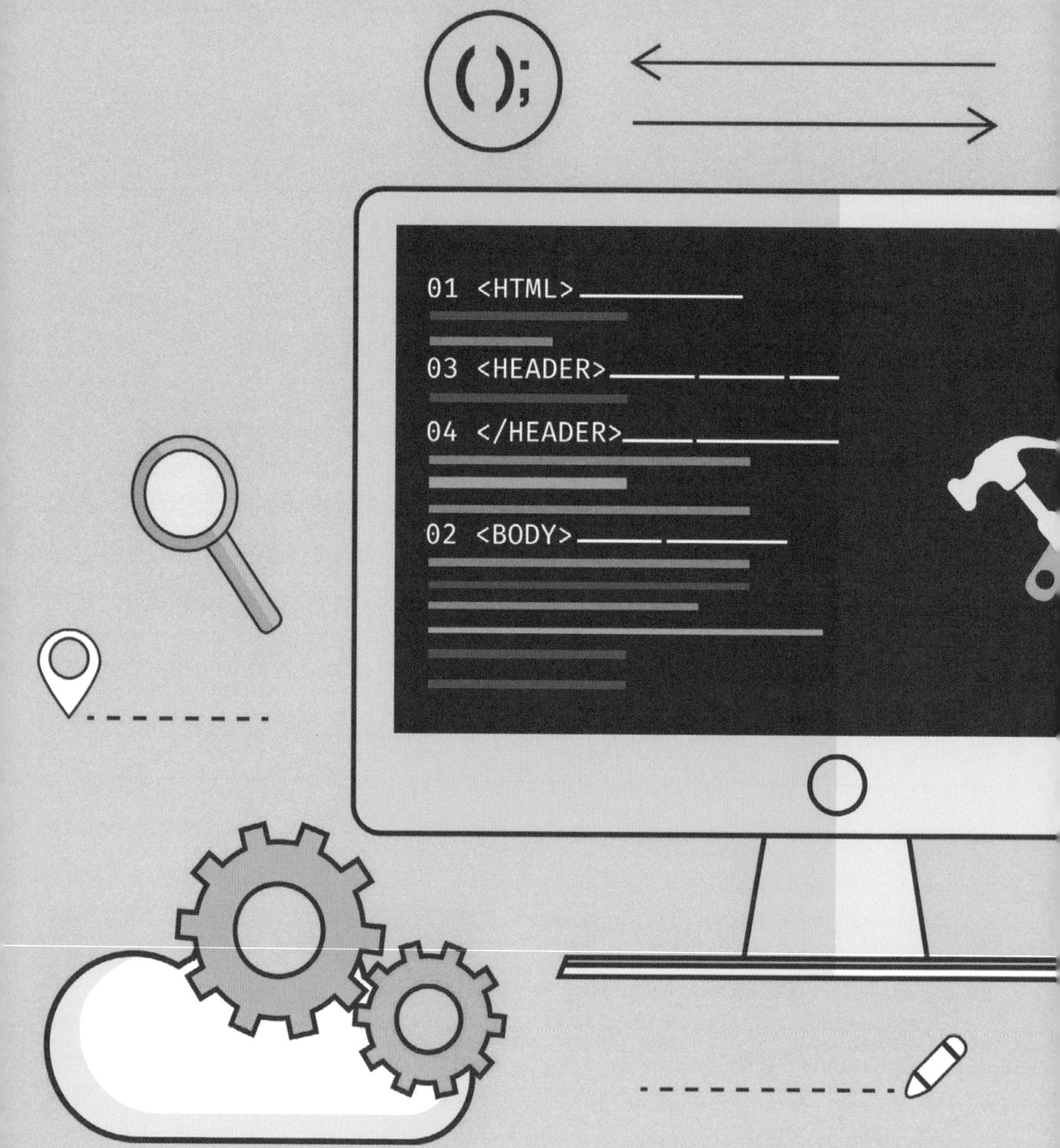

();
01 <HTML>
03 <HEADER>
04 </HEADER>
02 <BODY>

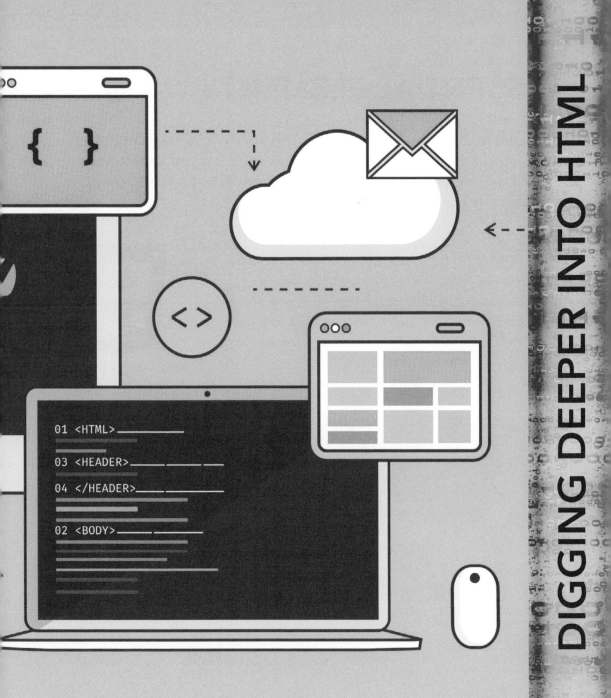

DIGGING DEEPER INTO HTML

ESSENTIAL ELEMENTS

In the last chapter, we looked at the main structural elements of HTML: `<head>`, `<body>`, `<main>`, `<article>` and so on. We also used elements for displaying text in headings and paragraphs. Let's now take a look at some more of HTML's essential elements.

HTML5

The current version of HTML, the one we're covering in this book, is called HTML5. HTML5 is in many ways very similar to older versions of the language, and it contains many of the elements found in those older versions. It also introduced a lot of new functionality that would previously have required plugins, such as Flash Player, to be installed on the user's browser.

Above: HTML5 is the latest and the greatest version of the language.

Above: If you want your pages to work properly on mobile device browsers, then HTML5 is the only game in town.

Better for Mobile

One of the main problems fixed by HTML5 is that many popular browser plugins cannot be installed on mobile operating systems. By removing the need for these plugins, HTML5 has ensured it's the only game in town for those who expect their pages to be viewed on mobile devices.

HTML5 SEMANTICS

Another issue with older versions of HTML was the lack of something called **semantic logic**. Semantics is all about conveying meaning within a logical structure... wow, what does that mean? Well, for example, many of the structural elements we've looked at so far – `<header>`, `<main>`, `<footer>`, and so on – didn't exist before HTML5.

Right: HTML5 strives to impose a logical structure where previously there was a free-for-all.

So to achieve the same result in older versions of HTML a developer's only option would be to use the special < d i v > element (*see* opposite). But 'div' conveys no meaning: it could be a page section, an article, or anything else; in short, 'div' is not semantic, whereas header, footer, article and so on are semantic.

Deciphering Bad Code

Not everybody writes good code, and we all make mistakes: all it takes is one missed closing tag, a typing error, a gap in knowledge or any number of other slip-ups, and the result may be an improperly formed HTML document. Because of this, web browsers have to be very good at making sense of such errors, and the introduction of semantics into the language makes it much easier for them to decipher badly formed HTML.

A FLEXIBLE FRIEND

Despite lacking any semantic meaning, `<div>` is a vital element that you will use regularly. `<div>` is unusual in that it has no specific intended use: it's an empty container that you can use for a variety of purposes, but its primary use is as a structural container for aiding page layout and for grouping related elements. At the heart of `<div>`'s flexibility lies CSS.

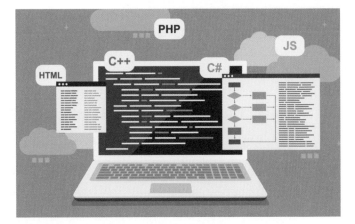

Hot Tip

The value given to an element's `id` attribute must not be used as the `id` for any other element within the same page.

The ID Attribute

You will recall that elements have attributes that can be assigned a value (*see page 19*). One such attribute, available to all visual elements, is `id`. This allows us to give a unique identifier to a specific element in a page and to target style rules at that element using a CSS **ID selector** (we discuss ID selectors on page 120).

```
26      <section id="leftPanel">
27          <div id="commandConsoleWrapper">
28              <div id="commandConsole">
29                  <p id="messagePanel" class="commsField"></p>
30                  <p id="currentScorePanel" class="commsField">0</p>
31                  <p id="bestScorePanel" class="commsField">100</p>
32              </div>
33          </div>
```

Above: Setting an element's `id` attribute allows that element to be targeted by CSS ID selectors.

Div's Dubious Semantics

The style rule(s) applied to a `<div>` element will determine how that `<div>` is displayed onscreen. Therefore with older versions of HTML, developers would generally use `<div>` elements to create

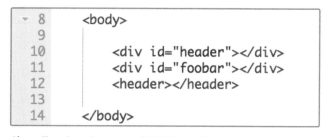

```
▼   8        <body>
    9
   10            <div id="header"></div>
   11            <div id="foobar"></div>
   12            <header></header>
   13
   14        </body>
```

Above: These three elements are valid HTML5 and will deliver identical visual results, but only one has semantic meaning.

the header, main, footer, etc. structure of a page – for example `<div id="header">`. But whilst an `id` value of 'header' may itself suggest some semantic logic, it could just as easily be set to foobar and achieve the same *visual* result but without the *semantic* meaning. Thus whilst the pre-HTML5 approach is still *valid* HTML5, it isn't *good* HTML5, so always favour HTML5 semantic elements, if available, over `<div>`.

HEADING SEMANTICS

We've already played around with some headings – <h1>, <h2>, and so on – and know that the different heading levels give different degrees of visual prominence. HTML5 goes a step further and imposes semantic meaning on the different heading levels; in other words, headings should help to define the logical structure of a page.

Hot Tip

Heading semantics can be tricky, but keep the book analogy in mind: it helps!

The easiest way to explain this is using the analogy of a book such as the one you are reading now. If a web page were a chapter in the book, then <h1> would be like the chapter title (such as on page 64), and so should only appear once in a web page.

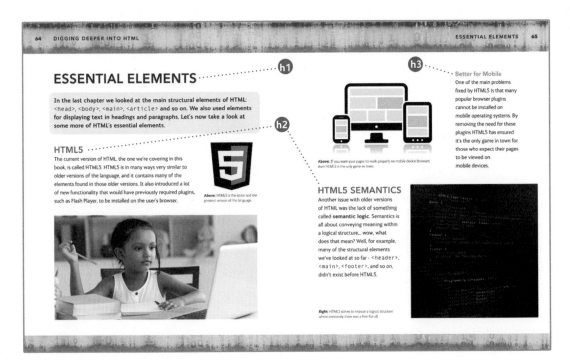

Above: Like the heading levels in a book, HTML5 headings give a logical structure to the text.

<h2> would be similar to section headings within a chapter, and so can appear more than once after a <h1>. <h3> would relate to all subheadings within a section, and so on.

Logical Structure of Headings

In HTML5, the different heading levels create a semantic structure; sticking with the book analogy, a subheading (<h3>) will have a parent section heading (<h2>), and that section heading will have a parent chapter heading (<h1>). But what if you want to create a single heading that has two components: a main heading and strapline, so to speak?

```
10    <h1>Level-1 Heading</h1>
11    <p>A level-1 heading is like the chapter heading in a book and so appears only once per page</p>
12    <h2>Level-2 Heading</h2>
13    <p>A level-2 heading is like a section within a chapter, and can appear numerous times following a level-1 heading.</p>
14    <h3>Level-3 Heading</h3>
15    <p>Level-3 headings are like sub-headings within a section. They can appear numerous times following a level-2 heading.</p>
16    <p>It would break the heading semantics if a level-3 heading was a direct child of a level-1 heading.</p>
17    <h4>Level-4 Heading</h4>
18    <p>You should have the idea by now: Level-4 headings can appear after a level-3 heading...</p>
19    <p>...and so on, all the way to level-6 headings.</p>
20
```

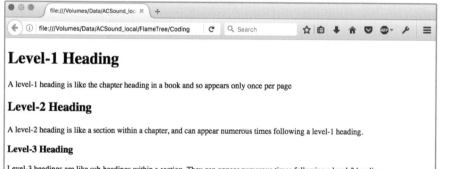

Left:
Although headings aren't nested within each other in the way elements are, they still define a logical structure.

Heading Groups

We might create a two-part heading like this:

```
<h1>It's Big News</h1>
<h2>Read All About It</h2>
```

Unfortunately, there's a problem here: the `<h2>` is being used as a subheading of `<h1>`, but it's also indicating a new section in the semantic structure of the page. To fix this, we use the `<hgroup>` element; this allows us to group together multiple levels of heading without implying that we're creating new sections in the semantic structure. The first heading in the `<hgroup>` is used to determine the semantic structure. So instead of the above, we would write:

```
<hgroup>
    <h1>It's Big News</h1>
    <h2>Read All About It</h2>
</hgroup>
```

Now the `<h2>` element will be seen as part of the `<h1>`, and semantic wellbeing is restored.

```
 9
10        <!--Semanitcally incorrect...:-->
11        <h1>HTML Heading Semantics</h1>
12        <h2>Easy When You Know How</h2>
13
14        <!--Semantically correct...:-->
15        <hgroup>
16            <h1>HTML Heading Semantics</h1>
17            <h2>Easy When You Know How</h2>
18        </hgroup>
19
```

Above: An `<hgroup>` element assists in maintaining semantic accuracy of headings.

LISTS

Lists are used a lot in web design. There are two basic list types, **unordered** and **ordered**, both of which will contain one or more **list items**. A third type, the **definition list**, creates a glossary-like structure of titles and associated information.

Hot Tip

It's common practice to use a `<ul>` element to provide a site's navigation menu (typically within a `<nav>` element). The `<ul>` can be styled to render its items horizontally or vertically.

```
10      <h2>Things To Do</h2>
11      <ul>
12          <li>Clean room</li>
13          <li>Do homework</li>
14          <li>Have tea</li>
15          <li>Enact plan for world domination</li>
16      </ul>
17
18      <h2>Plan For World Domination</h2>
19      <ol>
20          <li>Learn about coding</li>
21          <li>Develop a killer app</li>
22          <li>Sell killer app to everyone on planet</li>
23          <li>Get stinking rich</li>
24          <li>Buy volcanic island</li>
25          <li>Hollow out volcano and build secret lair within it</li>
26          <li>Demand everbody buys a 2nd copy of killer app to fund next volcano lair</li>
27      </ol>
```

Things To Do

- Clean room
- Do homework
- Have tea
- Enact plan for world domination

Plan For World Domination

1. Learn about coding
2. Develop a killer app
3. Sell killer app to everyone on planet
4. Get stinking rich
5. Buy volcanic island
6. Hollow out volcano and build secret lair within it
7. Demand everbody buys a 2nd copy of killer app to fund next volcano lair

List Items

Before looking at the list elements themselves, let's consider what goes into a list: the list item elements, `<li>`. Typically these contain text, but can contain pretty much anything you like: images (see page 84), hyperlinks (page 75) and, indeed, other lists. `<li>` elements are rendered in the order in which they appear in the parent list element.

Left: Lists allow us to present information in a structured and logical manner.

Unordered Lists

An unordered list, `<ul>`, is a simple bullet-point list. Each `<li>` element within the list creates a new bullet point. The `list-style-type` and `list-style-image` style properties allow you to change the appearance of the bullet-point markers.

Ordered Lists

In an ordered list, `<ol>`, each item is marked with a number or letter, which increases for each item. Interestingly, the style of numbering is determined by the `list-style-type` style property, the same property used to set the appearance of a `<ul>` list's bullet points. This shows that the only actual difference between `<ul>` and `<ol>` is in the default styling that's applied.

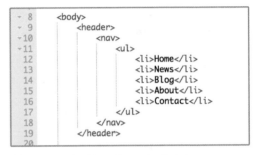

Above: An unordered list is often used as the basis of a site's navigation menu.

Definition Lists

A definition list, `<dl>`, is a bit like a glossary: each item consists of a title and a block of information relating to the title. This means that each item in the list actually has two components: A `<dt>` element for the title and a `<dd>` element for the information (the second 'd' representing the word 'data').

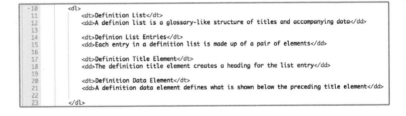

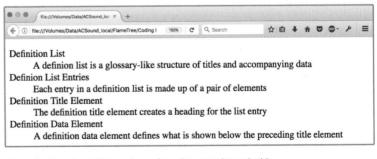

Above: Each item in a `<dl>` is made up of two elements: `<dt>` and `<dd>`.

```
10    <ul>
11        <li>
12            There are three types of HTML list:
13            <ul>
14                <li>Unordered lists</li>
15                <li>Ordered lists</li>
16                <li>Definition lists</li>
17            </ul>
18        </li>
19        <li>Ordered and unordered lists contain list item elements</li>
20        <li>
21            Definition lists contain paired title and data elements:
22            <dl>
23                <dt>Definition Title</dt>
24                <dd>The definition title element creates a heading above a definition data element</dd>
25                <dt>Pairs of elements</dt>
26                <dd>Each title element has an accompanying data element</dd>
27            </dl>
28        </li>
29        <li>
30            Unordered and ordered lists vary only in the sybmol they use for marking each item - remember:
31            <ol>
32                <li>Ordered lists show a numeral or letter marker that increases for each list item</li>
33                <li>Unordered lists show a bullet point marker that is the same for each list item</li>
34                <li>The difference is purely down to the list-style-type style property</li>
35            </ol>
36        </li>
37        <li>
38            Lists can be...
39            <ul>
40                <li>...nested inside...</li>
41                <li>...other lists, which themselves...</li>
42                <ol>
43                    <li>...can be nested within...</li>
```

Lists Within Lists

If you wish to create a multi-level list, the solution is to place a new list element within a < l i > or <dd> element. You can do this with any of the three list types, and you can mix and match the different types as required.

Above: You can add lists inside other lists in order to create a multi-tiered or multi-level list.

HYPERLINKS

A website would not be a website if it didn't have hyperlinks; they are the mechanism that allow any web browsing to happen at all, and without them there would be no way to navigate within a site, or to direct people to external sites. A website would be nothing more than a single, static page.

The Anchor Element

At the heart of the hyperlink mechanism lies the anchor element, < a >. It's called this because one of its uses is for marking specific points, or anchors, in a page. This use remains, but < a > is more commonly used for creating hyperlinks to other pages.

Left: Without hyperlinks there would be no such thing as Google... think on that for a while...!

Creating a Hyperlink

We create a hyperlink by wrapping an
<a> element's opening and closing tags
around the text we want to convert
into a hyperlink: the URL (see page 58)
that you want to link to is given
as the value of the <a> element's
href attribute.

Hot Tip

If using hyperlinks to open other
pages in your own site, you can
use relative URLs rather than
absolute URLs (see page 58).

Opening a Hyperlink in a New Window

It's often desirable to open a hyperlink in a new browser window so that your own page or site
remains open in the background. This is done via the target attribute of the <a> element,
like this:

```
<a href="http://www.flametreepublishing.com" target="_blank">
```

```
11
12          <p>Visit our <a href="http://www.flametreepublishing.com">homepage</a> now</p>
13
```

Above: We use an <a> element to create a hyperlink by wrapping it around the text to be linked.

TABLES

Once upon a time, HTML tables were used for controlling the layout of a web page. CSS came along and put an end to such nonsense, but tables remain an important weapon in the web developer's armory.

As a topic, HTML tables can become very complicated and fiddly, but a lot of that complexity is a hangover from when they were used for page layout purposes. If all you wish to do is present some basic information in a tabular (i.e. table-like) form, then much of the complexity can be ignored.

Table Elements

Tables are made up of a number of different elements, all nested within an outer `<table>` element. The order of the elements is important if the table is to be correctly formed.

Pokémon	Type	Ability
Pikachu	Electric	Static
Charmander	Fire	Blaze
Squirtle	Water	Torrent
Bulbasaur	Grass, Poison	Overgrow
Eevee	Normal	Run Away, Adaptability
Snorlax	Normal	Thick Fat, Immunity

Above: Once used for laying out pages, tables are now mainly used for presenting information, which is what they were designed for in the first place!

Table Header and Body

< table > elements contain header and body elements: < thead > and < tbody >. The table header contains the headings that sit above each column, whilst the table body contains the actual information being displayed by the table. You don't have to include a header in a table, or indeed a < tbody > element, although without a body section, it's hard to see why you'd want to use a table!

Table Rows

Within the < thead > and < tbody > elements, we place table row elements: < tr > (a row is a horizontal line of entries in the table).

Table head <thead>

Book Title	Author	Publisher	ISBN
Coding for Kids	Adam Crute	Flame Tree Publishing	978-1-78664-540-1
C Programming – A Modern Approach	K.N. King	W.W. Norton	978-0-393-97950-3
Learning Python	Mark Lutz	O'Reilly	978-1-449-35573-9
Teach Yourself SQL	Ben Forta	Sams Publishing	0-672-32567-5

Table body <tbody>

Table rows <tr>

Table cells <td>

Table Cells

Finally, within the `<tr>` elements, we define the **cells** of the table – in other words the individual containers that will hold table entries. Table cells are defined using `<td>` element ('td' stands for table data). It's up to the developer to ensure that each `<tr>` element in a table contains the same number of `<td>` elements.

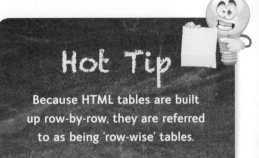

Hot Tip

Because HTML tables are built up row-by-row, they are referred to as being 'row-wise' tables.

Table Example

We'll be making use of tables in Chapter 5: Playing With Code (*see page 198*), so we'll get some practice in there. In the meantime, by way of example, take a look at the image on the right to see the HTML that creates a table; why not copy it into your own HTML document and have a play around with the code?

Right: The HTML for a complete table looks like this.

```
27  <table>
28      <thead>
29          <tr>
30              <td>Book Title</td>
31              <td>Author</td>
32              <td>Publisher</td>
33              <td>ISBN number</td>
34          </tr>
35      </thead>
36      <tbody>
37          <tr>
38              <td>Coding For Kids</td>
39              <td>Adam Crute</td>
40              <td>Flametree Publishing</td>
41              <td>TBC</td>
42          </tr>
43          <tr>
44              <td>C Programming - A modern approach</td>
45              <td>K N King</td>
46              <td>W. W. Norton</td>
47              <td>978-0-393-97950-3</td>
48          </tr>
49          <tr>
50              <td>Learning Python</td>
51              <td>Mark Lutz</td>
52              <td>O'Reilly</td>
53              <td>978-1-449-35573-9</td>
54          </tr>
55          <tr>
56              <td>Teach Yourself SQL</td>
57              <td>Ben Forta</td>
58              <td>Sams Publishing</td>
59              <td>0-672-32567-5</td>
60          </tr>
61      </tbody>
62
63
64  </table>
```

IMAGES

Alongside text, images are the element that almost every website has in common. Very rarely will you find a modern web page that totally lacks imagery. Images are extremely versatile and have the potential to make a page much more visually appealing.

Image Formats

Images come in a variety of formats, but on the web, there are effectively four used: GIF, PNG, JPG and SVG. The GIF format has fallen out of favour, as the image quality tends to be poor (although the ability to create animated GIFs keeps them hanging on). PNG and JPG, on the other hand, are widely used, and SVG is increasingly common. All have specific advantages and disadvantages, but together they can satisfy all situations.

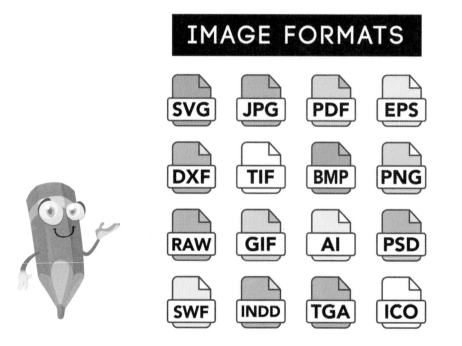

Above: We can use various formats of image in our web pages: JPG for photos, and PNG or SVG for graphics.

Hot Tip

When creating images and graphics, work from a full-quality, editable version in a lossless format such as PSD (Photoshop's native format) or AI (Illustrator's native format), then export the elements you need as PNG, JPG and/or SVG files.

The PNG Format

PNG (Portable Network Graphics, pronounced ping) are a good option for graphics, but less useful for photographic imagery due to them having larger file sizes than JPG; that additional file size, however, makes for a better-quality image. They also benefit from supporting transparency – in other words a PNG image needn't have a solid-coloured background, and anything behind them can show through the transparent areas of the PNG.

The JPG Format

The JPG format (also known as JPEG, pronounced jay-peg) uses an advanced data compression technique to reduce the file size of an image without visibly degrading the picture quality.

Above: Transparent areas of a PNG image allow anything behind the image to show through.

You can adjust the quality level when saving, allowing you to balance the file size against the image quality. JPGs don't support transparency, and their compression techniques are not 'lossless'; they are best suited to photographs and larger images.

The SVG Format

SVG stands for Scalable Vector Graphics. Unlike **bitmapped** images like PNG and JPG, in which each pixel of an image is directly represented by color data in the image file, **vector** graphics describe the lines, curves, fills and colours of a graphic in mathematical terms. This results in a graphic that has a very small file size, and the image size can be increased without losing any quality or sharpness.

Above: Vector graphics can be scaled without becoming pixelated or blocky.

EXERCISE 5: **ADDING IMAGES**

In the previous chapter, we created a basic text-only page. We're going to enhance this now with some images, and take a look at different ways of placing and positioning them.

THE IMAGE ELEMENT

To add an image to a page, we use the `<img>` element. This is a self-closing element meaning, as you will recall, it only has an opening tag and no closing tag, and can't have any elements nested within it.

`<img>` is what's known as an **inline** element (*see* page 144). This means, amongst other things, that the browser will render it without breaking the content flow of the parent element.

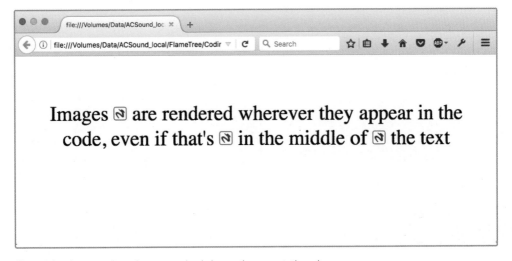

Above: Inline elements such as `<img>` are rendered wherever they appear in the code.

For example, if an <img> element is placed *between* two <p> elements, a gap will be created between the paragraphs, and the image will be displayed in that gap. If, however, an <img> is placed *inside* a <p> element, it will be drawn at that point in the flow of text, and it won't create breaks or carriage returns within the text.

Image Element Attributes

The <img> element has a couple of attributes that we need to set. The most important is src, which is where we specify the image's filename as a URL. The other is alt: this is a short description of the image and is used by screenreader applications for the visually impaired, as well as being shown if the image fails to load.

Hot Tip

There are a number of photo libraries on the internet. Shutterstock (www.shutterstock.com) is good for commercial images, whilst Pexels (www.pexels.com) is a great source of license- and royalty-free images.

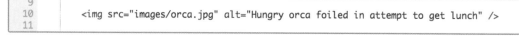

```
 9
10          <img src="images/orca.jpg" alt="Hungry orca foiled in attempt to get lunch" />
11
```

Above: The src attribute tells the browser where to grab the image from; the alt attribute adds a short description to an image.

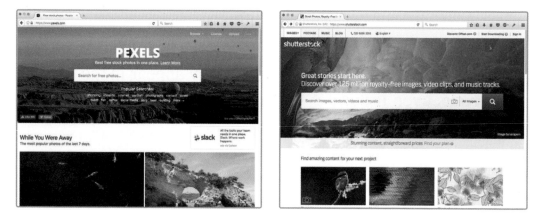

Above: Photo libraries are a great source of images for your website.

PREPARING IMAGES

1. For this exercise we're going to continue from where we left off in the last exercise. If you haven't done that exercise then you can copy the files and folders from the Exercise5\ startingPoint\, contained in the downloadable code package, to your project folder.

2. If not using our starting point then you need to find some images to help illustrate the information on your page. Choose an image to illustrate the About section of your page and then open it in your image editor.

Above: Open your 'About' section picture in your image editor.

3. We need to size the image so that it's a good fit for our page. Some editors allow you to resize an image at the same time as exporting to JPG, but others require you to first resize the image and then Export/ Save As the image. For our purposes we need an image that's no bigger than 400 x 300 pixels in size.

Above: Affinity Photo allows you to resize and export your image in one simple step; Photoshop has similar functionality, but in GIMP it's a two-step process.

4. When exporting or saving a JPG, you will be able to adjust the JPG compression quality: the higher the quality, the bigger the file size and so the slower the image will download. You need to judge how best to set the compression quality, balancing file size (and therefore download time) against image quality; for this image, aim for a file size of around 30kb.

Above: Use the JPG compression setting to balance file size against image quality.

5. Export/Save the JPG into a new subfolder of your MyFirstWebPage folder; call the subfolder Images and the file aboutImage.jpg. It's good practice to avoid spaces and punctuation other than underscores _ when naming any file for use in a web page.

Above: Save the image to an Images subfolder of the MyFirstWebPage folder.

ADDING THE 'ABOUT' IMAGE TO YOUR PAGE

1. Open MyFirstWebPage.htm in your HTML editor. Locate the `<script>` element and delete it, as we don't need it at the moment.

2. Scroll back up the page and locate the `<section>` element that contains the About heading. Underneath the `<h2>` heading element, add the following, replacing `"yourImageDescription"` with something appropriate for your picture:

   `<img src="images/aboutImage.jpg" alt="yourImageDescription" />`

```
22      <main>
23          <section>
24              <h2>About</h2>
25              <img src="images/aboutImage.jpg" alt="SpiderPenguin out-stares a seal" />
26              <p>Following an accident involving kelp, toxic waste, a nuclear submarine and a tasty tuna fish, r
```

Above: Add the image element after the heading element.

3. Save the page and open it in your browser. As you may have expected, the image appears between the heading and the paragraph text. Let's try a different way of positioning it.

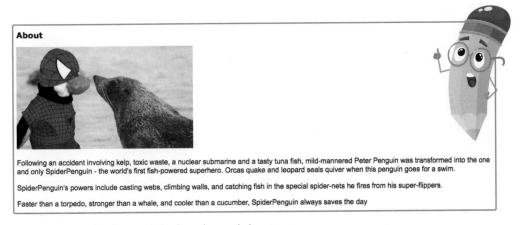

Above: The image is placed between the heading and paragraph element.

4. Return to your code editor/IDE. Select the `<img>` element and use cut-and-paste to move it inside the first `<p>` element of the section, placing it before the text.

```
▾22          <main>
▾23              <section>
 24                  <h2>About</h2>
 25                  <p><img src="images/aboutImage.jpg" alt="SpiderPenguin out-stares a seal" />Following an accident ir
      kaln  toxic wocto  o nucloon cuhmorino ond o tocty tuno fich  mild-monnored Poter Donauin wac troncformed into the c
```

Above: Move the `<img>` element inside the first `<p>`.

5. Save the page and open it in your browser again. This time, you will see the image is sitting in line with the first line of paragraph text, but the bottom of the image is aligned to the text **baseline**, so the text aligns with the bottom of the image. It would look much better if the text started at the top of the image and ran alongside it...

About

Following an accident involving kelp, toxic w mild-mannered Peter Penguin was transformed into the one and only SpiderPenguin - the world's firs seals quiver when this penguin goes for a swim.

SpiderPenguin's powers include casting webs, climbing walls, and catching fish in the special spider-

Faster than a torpedo, stronger than a whale, and cooler than a cucumber, SpiderPenguin always sa

Above: The image is now in line with the text, but it still doesn't look right (notice where the text starts).

FLOATING AND PADDING THE IMAGE

We often want text to flow around an image, and this is achieved with something called **floating**. When we 'float' an image, we are telling the browser to place the image to one side or the other of its **sibling** elements.

1. Floating is applied using the float style property, which takes a value of left, right or none. Open MyFirstCSS.css in your editor, add a new line at the end of the sheet and add the following selector and style rule:

```
img {
    float: left;
}
```

2. Save your work and open the page in your browser. The text now flows around the image: nice! If we gave it a float value of right then it would be placed at the right of the screen despite being coded as the first thing in the <p> element (why not try it and see for yourself).

> ## Hot Tip
>
> We've already learned that elements have a parent element, and that many elements have child elements; 'sibling' elements, then, are elements that share the same parent.

About

Following an accident involving kelp, toxic waste, a nuclear submarine and a tasty tuna fish, mild-mannered Peter Penguin was transformed into the one and only SpiderPenguin - the world's first fish-powered superhero. Orcas quake and leopard seals quiver when this penguin goes for a swim.

SpiderPenguin's powers include casting webs, climbing walls, and catching fish in the special spider-nets he fires from his super-flippers.

Faster than a torpedo, stronger than a whale, and cooler than a cucumber, SpiderPenguin always saves the day

Above: Floating the image makes the text flow around it.

3. We could do with a bit of space between the image and the text. There are a few different ways to do this, which we discuss on page 134, but one way is to apply **padding** to one or more sides of the < img > element.

4. We want a gap to the right and underneath our image, so flip back to MyFirstCSS.css in your code editor and update the img selector's style rule so it looks like this:

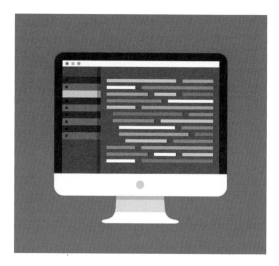

```
img {
    float: left;
    padding-right: 12px;
    padding-bottom: 12px;
}
```

About

Following an accident involving kelp, toxic waste, a nuclear submarine and a tasty tuna fish, mild-mannered Peter Penguin was transformed into the one and only SpiderPenguin - the world's first fish-powered superhero. Orcas quake and leopard seals quiver when this penguin goes for a swim.

SpiderPenguin's powers include casting webs, climbing walls, and catching fish in the special spider-nets he fires from his super-flippers.

Faster than a torpedo, stronger than a whale, and cooler than a cucumber, SpiderPenguin always saves the day

Above: Padding is one way of creating some space around an image.

5. Save your work and open the page in your browser. Great job – the image is showing, and the text is flowing around it whilst leaving a bit of space around the edge of the image.

VIDEO AND AUDIO IN WEB PAGES

HTML5 introduced `<video>` and `<audio>` elements to the language. These make it much easier to include such media in your pages and sites than it was with the previous approach of embedding third-party players that required browser plugins in order to work.

VIDEO

Video is widely used in web pages and sites: it is attention-grabbing and much more engaging than a static image. Videos can also get across more information than static images and text occupying the same space on the page.

Above: Including videos can really bring your pages to life.

HOSTING YOUR OWN VIDEO FILES

Video files tend to have a large filesize, which is a nuisance when it comes to delivering them over the internet.

If you host the video files on a web server, you need to be sure that your server's internet connection can handle delivering such large files to the expected number of site visitors. Also, some server providers will set a limit on the amount of data that can be downloaded from the server each month before additional charges are applied, so you have to beware that you don't end up over-using this data allowance or things could get expensive! (Our examples will run from your computer, so you're safe when working on the exercises).

Above: If you put your videos on a web server, be careful that you don't run up unexpected server charges if lots of people come and view your video.

Video CODECs

Video compatibility can be a bit confusing. Firstly, all digital video uses data compression of some form or other; this is called the CODEC (which stands for En**co**de/**Dec**ode). Your choice of CODEC could impact on which browsers or operating systems can open the video.

Video File Types

Things get more confusing when you add in the various different file types that can contain video; again, not all file types are compatible with all browsers and/or operating systems.

Helpful HTML

Thankfully, help is at hand. Firstly, HTML5's `<video>` element allows more than one source file to be defined, leaving the user's browser to select the version it's compatible with. Secondly, there are nowadays three CODEC/file combinations that are becoming standardized and so are widely supported.

Common Video CODEC and File-type Combinations

- H.264 CODEC in MP4 file
- Theora CODEC in OGG file
- VP8 or VP9 CODEC in WebM file

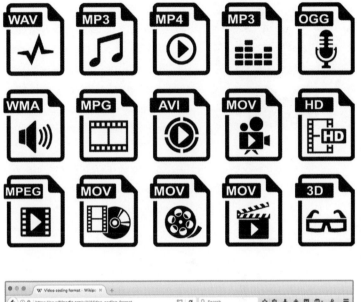

Above: If you want to learn more about video compression and file types, Wikipedia is a good place to start.

Converting Videos

There are various tools and applications that can produce video in, or convert it to, one of the web-standard video formats. One of the best is HandBrake (https://handbrake.fr/), a free cross-platform tool that does an excellent job of converting video to H.264/MP4 format. The enormous number of settings on offer can be baffling, but HandBrake provides a number of presets for dealing with common conversion tasks.

A simple way of converting to Ogg and WebM is to use VideoLAN VLC Player (www.videolan.org). This free cross-platform media player has a Convert/Stream function that can convert your video to a number of different video formats.

Above: HandBrake is an excellent tool for converting videos to MP4.

EXERCISE 6: CREATING A VIDEO PLAYER PAGE

Let's have a play around with adding a video player to a web page. We have provided an example video that you can use in the following exercise; alternatively you can use a video of your own if you have something suitable to hand.

USING THE <VIDEO> ELEMENT

1. Create a new project folder and call it MyMediaPlayer.

2. If you wish to use our supplied videos, then open the Exercise6\startingPoint\MyMediaPlayer\ folder from within the downloadable code package, and copy the video folder from there to your own MyMediaPlayer project folder. If using your own videos then create a video folder in your MyMediaPlayer folder and save your videos to this folder.

Above: Create a project folder; place your videos into a subfolder called video.

3. Create a new HTML file inside MyMediaPlayer and save it as MyVideoPlayer.htm.

4. Open the new HTML file in your code editor/IDE and add the basic HTML structural elements <!DOCTYPE>, <html>, <head> and <body>.

Right: Don't forget, all of your HTML documents should start like this.

```
1  <!DOCTYPE html>
2
3  <html>
4
5      <head>
6      </head>
7
8      <body>
9      </body>
10
11
12  </html>
```

5. Create a couple of empty lines within the `<body>` element and then, still within `<body>`, add a basic video element, `<video>`.

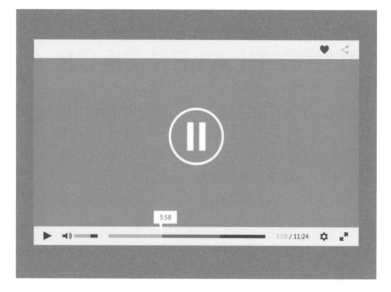

6. The HTML video element has the ability to point to multiple video files, but for now, let's stick with linking to just one video file. Add a `src` attribute to the `<video>` element's opening tag, and provide the URL of your video as the attribute value. For example, if using the MP4 video we've provided, the opening tag will look like this:

```
<video src="video/StonehamSentinelSS1.mp4">
```

If you are using your own video, replace `StonehamSentinelSS1.mp4` with the filename of your video.

```
 8    <body>
 9
10        <video src="video/StonehamSentinelSS1.mp4"></video>
11
12    </body>
```

Above: Your `<video>` element should look something like this.

7. We need to inform the browser what type of video we're passing it. We do this with the `type` attribute. If your video is an MP4 file then the value for `type` should be `"video/mp4"`; for WebM, it's `"video/webm"`; and for Ogg, it's `"video/ogg"`. We'll add this attribute now. We're using an MP4 video, so our opening tag should look like this:

```
<video src="video/StonehamSentinelSS1.mp4" type="video/mp4">
```

```
▾ 8     <body>
  9
  10        <video src="video/StonehamSentinelSS1.mp4" type="video/mp4"></video>
  11
  12    </body>
  13
```

Above: The type attribute lets the browser know what format of video to expect.

8. The `controls` attribute of the `<video>` element determines whether or not the browser will display a control bar on the video.

This is an unusual attribute because it doesn't actually require a value: if the attribute appears in the opening tag, then controls will be shown; if not, then no controls will be shown. That said, it's common practice to include a value of `"controls"`, if only to keep your IDE's error-checking from constantly flagging it up as a problem. Add the `controls` attribute to your `<video>` element:

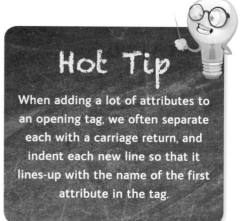

Hot Tip

When adding a lot of attributes to an opening tag, we often separate each with a carriage return, and indent each new line so that it lines-up with the name of the first attribute in the tag.

```
<video src="video/
StonehamSentinelSS1.mp4"

type="video/mp4"

controls="controls">
```

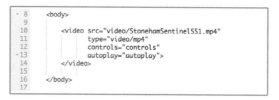

```
8    <body>
9
10       <video src="video/StonehamSentinelSS1.mp4"
11              type="video/mp4"
12              controls="controls">
13       </video>
14
15    </body>
16
```

Above: The `controls` attribute creates a control bar for the video player.

9. Another `<video>` element attribute that doesn't need a value is `autoplay`, which tells the browser to start playing the video as soon as it is able to. Go ahead and add this to your `<video>` element too:

```
8    <body>
9
10       <video src="video/StonehamSentinelSS1.mp4"
11              type="video/mp4"
12              controls="controls"
13              autoplay="autoplay">
14       </video>
15
16    </body>
17
```

Above: Your completed `<video>` opening tag should look something like this. Notice the way attributes have been listed on new indented lines.

```
<video src="video/StonehamSentinelSS1.mp4"
       type="video/mp4"
       controls="controls"
       autoplay="autoplay">
```

10. Save your work and open MyVideoPlayer. htm in your web browser. If your operating system and browser supports MP4 files, then the video will automatically load and play; if you roll your mouse over the video, then a control strip should appear at the bottom of the video player.

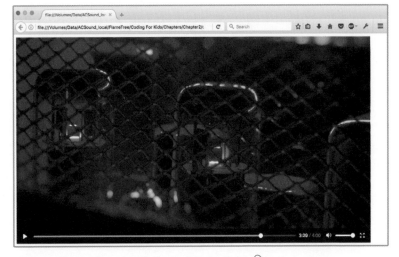

Above: The browser will create a video player and play the video.

The <source> Element

As mentioned, the <video> element can point to versions of a video prepared using different CODECs and file types. To do this we nest one or more <source> elements within the <video> element. We've included Ogg and WebM versions of our example video; if you're using your own video then create versions in both formats before continuing.

Name		Date Modified	Size	Kind
MyVideoPlayer.htm		Today, 13:27	515 bytes	HTML
▼ video		Today, 13:53	--	Folder
StonehamSentinelSS1.mp4		10 Jun 2017, 18:06	35.2 MB	MPEG-4 movie
StonehamSentinelSS1.ogg		Today, 13:15	39.2 MB	Ogg V...dio File
StonehamSentinelSS1.webm		Today, 13:51	27.9 MB	HTML...(WebM)

Above: We've provided the example video in MP4, Ogg and WebM formats.

USING THE \<SOURCE> ELEMENT

1. Open MyVideoPlayer.htm in your editor. Locate the `<video>` element and then select and cut ([ctrl]+[x] / [cmd]+[x]) the `src` and `type` attributes and their values.

2. Within the `<video>` element, i.e between its opening and closing tags, add a new `<source>` element (a self-closing element). Paste the attributes that you cut from the `<video>` element: you should end up with code like that shown below (you may need to tidy up the indenting of your opening tags).

3. Our alternative-version videos are in Ogg and WebM formats – add `<source>` elements for these:

```
<source src="video/StonehamSentinalSS1.ogg" type="video/ogg" />
<source src="video/StonehamStentinalSS1.webm" type="video/webm" />
```

```
 8   <body>
 9
10       <video controls="controls" autoplay="autoplay">
11           <source src="video/StonehamSentinelSS1.mp4" type="video/mp4"/>
12       </video>
13
14   </body>
15
```

Above: Cut-and-paste the `src` and `type` attributes into the new `<source>` element.

4. Save your work and open the page in your browser. You should see exactly the same as before; indeed, there is no easy way to tell which version of the video – MP4, Ogg or WebM – is

```
 8   <body>
 9
10       <video controls="controls" autoplay="autoplay">
11           <source src="video/StonehamSentinelSS1.mp4" type="video/mp4"/>
12           <source src="video/StonehamSentinelSS1.ogg" type="video/ogg"/>
13           <source src="video/StonehamSentinelSS1.webm" type="video/webm"/>
14       </video>
15
16   </body>
17
```

Above: The `<video>` element now defines three possible source videos; the browser will choose the first it can work with.

Above: By including multiple versions of the video, we can be sure it will work on as many browsers and operating systems as possible.

being played. However, you can rest easy in the knowledge that it is now unlikely that a visitor to your page will be unable to view your video.

Hot Tip

The most widely supported video format is H.264 in an MP4 file, so always provide a version of your video using this CODEC and file type.

Keep it Legal

Be cautious about what videos you publish from your own web server; if you don't own the copyright to a video, or don't have permission to publish from the people featured in a video, then you could be breaking the law!

AUDIO

Audio may not be as widely used on the web as video, but it can be important for some pages and sites, especially the sites of musicians and music publishers. As far as HTML is concerned, audio is very similar to video, and so there is very little difference in how the two elements work.

The <audio> Element

You can work with the <audio> element in much the same way as you do the <video> element. The only real difference is that if you don't set the controls attribute of an <audio> element then that element will have no visual output at all, and the only way to control the playback would be via JavaScript.

Above: The <audio> element allows musicians to publish their own music online.

EMBEDDING CONTENT FROM OTHER SITES

There are all sorts of services out there on the internet: video and music streaming, social media, news feeds, and so on, and many allow you to embed their content into your own web page. In the case of video, this is often far easier than hosting your own video files.

The <iframe> Element

When embedding content from external websites, the most commonly used mechanism is the <iframe> element. The <iframe> code is provided by the external site, and allows that site to, in effect, take control of an area of your page. If this sounds quite drastic, then it's because it is! Whoever controls that external site can, and normally will, gather information about the people who visit your page.

If the external site is run by people with bad intentions, or if it is hacked in some way, then your page and its visitors could become infected with malware. It is therefore vital that you only include < i f r ame > elements from sources you trust completely.

Video Sharing Services

One of the best ways to include your own video in your page is by uploading it to a video sharing service such as YouTube or Vimeo, and then using an < i f r ame > embed code from that service to make the video appear in your own page. As well as saving you from the need to ensure your web server can cope with delivering video, it also means your video will be available to a much wider audience via the YouTube (or whatever) site.

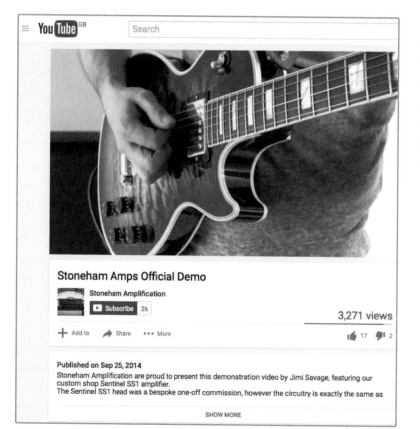

Left: YouTube is the world's biggest video sharing site.

EXERCISE 7: **EMBEDDING A YOUTUBE VIDEO**

In the last exercise, we learned how to display video that was hosted on your own web server. Now let's see how to do it using a YouTube embed code.

CREATE A GOOGLE ACCOUNT

If you want to upload your own video to YouTube, then you will need a Google account. If you already have one then great, you're good to go; if not, then pop along to https://accounts.google.com/SignUp and work through the signup procedure, it only takes a couple of minutes.

Example Video

If you don't have a video to upload but would like to try embedding a YouTube video, then browse YouTube for a video you like and then jump forward to step 5 on page 107.

Right: Creating a Google account only takes a few minutes.

UPLOADING TO YOUTUBE

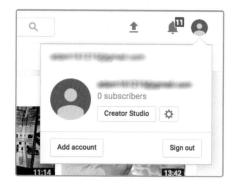

1. Head over to www.youtube.com and log in to your Google account. Once logged in, click the account button at the top-right of the page and click the Creator Studio button.

2. If you've never uploaded to YouTube before, then a big blue link will ask you to create a channel. Click the link and follow the onscreen instructions to create your new channel.

Above: Log in to your Google account from YouTube and then head to the Creator Studio.

3. Once your channel is set up, you will be returned to the YouTube dashboard. This gives an overview of the videos you have uploaded, the number of views they've received and so on.

Above: Create a channel if you don't already have one.

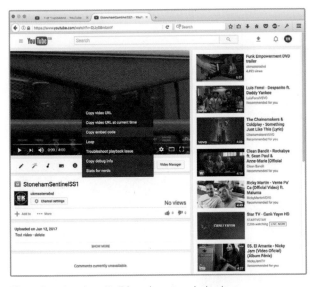

Above: Add some information about your video whilst it is uploading and processing.

Above: Open the video in YouTube and copy its embed code.

4. Click the Upload button at the top-right of the screen and then follow the onscreen instructions for uploading your video. You can add information about the video whilst it's uploading and processing. Once processing is complete, click the Done button, and then the Video Manager button to go to the Video Manager area of the Creator Studio.

5. In the Video Manager, click on your newly uploaded video to see it displayed on the normal YouTube site. From there, right-click on the video and select Copy embed code from the popup menu.

6. Open MyVideoPlayer.htm in your code editor and locate the `<video>` element. Before its opening tag, type: `<!--`, and after its closing tag, type `-->`.

7. What we have just done is **comment out** the current <video> element. Any section in an HTML document that's surrounded by an opening <!-- and closing --> comment marker will be ignored by the web browser. This is useful for adding notes and descriptions to your documents, as well as for disabling blocks of code, as we've just done.

```
 8    <body>
 9
10        <!--<video controls="controls" autoplay="autoplay">
11            <source src="video/StonehamSentinelSS1.mp4" type="video/mp4"/>
12            <source src="video/StonehamSentinelSS1.ogg" type="video/ogg"/>
13            <source src="video/StonehamSentinelSS1.webm" type="video/webm"/>
14        </video>-->
15
16    </body>
17
```

Above: Comment markers can be used to disable sections of code (notice how the IDE has made the code grey in colour).

8. Create a new line underneath the disabled <video> element and then paste the YouTube embed code, an <iframe> element, into your document. You can adjust the attributes of the <iframe> if you wish, but don't modify the src attribute.

9. Save your page and open it in your web browser. As you can see, you now have a YouTube-style video player window on your page. Also, if you pause the video or allow it to play to the end, YouTube will use the < i f r ame > element to show other videos from your channel, or other videos that YouTube has determined are similar to yours.

The Low-Risk Option

A lot of YouTube content will provide an embed code that you can use in your own site, so you aren't limited to linking to your own videos. Better still, if you are using an embedded YouTube (or Vimeo or whatever) < i f r ame > then you are not the publisher of the video and so can relax about those bothersome copyright issues.

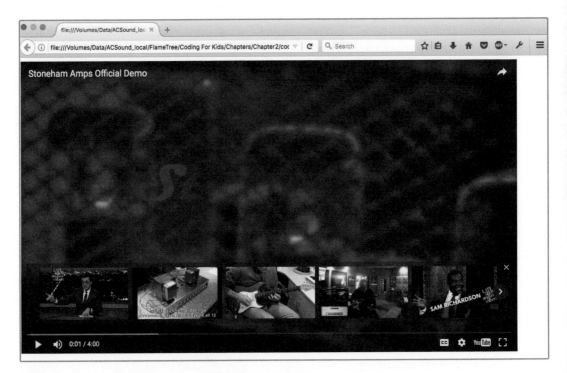

Above: You now have a YouTube player window embedded in your own web page.

DIGGING DEEPER INTO CSS

UNDERSTANDING CSS SELECTORS

We've already looked at CSS Type selectors, but there are other forms of selector too. It's also possible to combine selectors in various ways; let's take a look.

ID SELECTORS

An ID selector targets the single element whose `id` attribute value matches the ID selector. An ID selector looks like this:

```
#myElement { style rule }
```

The # (hash) states that this is an ID selector; its style rule will be applied to the HTML element whose id attribute value is `"myElement"`.

```
▾11      <main>
▾12          <section>
 13
 14              <p>This paragraph is using default styling.</p>
 15              <p id="specialPara">But this paragraph has specific styling targeted at it via an ID selector.</p>
 16              <p>Now, we're back to a default-styled paragraph.</p>
 17
 18          </section>
 19
 20      </main>
```

```
  4
▾ 5  #specialPara {
  6      font-weight: 700;
  7      font-size: 18px;
  8      color: blue;
  9  }
 10
```

This paragraph is using default styling.

But this paragraph has specific styling targeted at it via an ID selector.

Now, we're back to a default-styled paragraph.

Above: The ID selector allows a style rule to be targeted at a specific HTML element.

ID selectors have high specificity (*see* page 23); in other words, style properties defined in an ID selector's style rule will override the same style properties provided by Type and/or Class selectors.

CLASS SELECTORS

As you know, a Type selector targets any HTML elements with the same element name as the selector, and an ID selector targets the single HTML element with a matching `id` attribute value. A Class selector, then, allows you to target a specific classification of HTML elements. A Class selector is written like this (notice the fullstop which precedes the class name):

```
.myClassName { style rule }
```

This selector would target any and all HTML elements that had been given the classification of `myClassName`. But how do we classify an element? Read on.

The Class Attribute

Every visual element in HTML has a `class` attribute. Here's how it looks:

```
<article class="newsStory">
```

```
11      <main>
12          <section>
13
14              <p>This paragraph is using default styling.</p>
15              <p class="boldText">This paragraph is being styled by the 'boldText' class selector.</p>
16              <p class="italicText">And this paragraph is being styled by the 'italicText' class selector.</p>
17              <p>Now, we're back to a default-styled paragraph.</p>
18
19          </section>
20
21      </main>
```

Above: HTML elements can be given classifications via the class attribute.

```
 2
 3  .boldText {
 4      font-weight: 700;
 5  }
 6
 7  .italicText {
 8      font-style: italic;
 9  }
10
```

```
file:///Volumes/Data/ACSound_loc  ×   +
file:///Volumes/Data/ACSound_local/Flame    C    Q Search

This paragraph is using default styling.

This paragraph is being styled by the 'boldText' class selector.

And this paragraph is being styled by the 'italicText' class selector.

Now, we're back to a default-styled paragraph.
```

Above: HTML elements can be given classifications via the class attribute – see how they appear on the webpage.

Once given a classification in this way, the element will receive the style rule associated with the `.newsStory` CSS selector.

Multiple Classifications

Imagine you have created three different Class selectors in a page's CSS: `.boldText`, `.italicText` and `.underlinedText`, and assigned a suitable style rule to each, such as `{font-weight: 700;}` etc. You could then classify text-based elements using these class names in order to change the styling of those elements.

```
11      <main>
12          <section>
13
14              <p>This paragraph is using default styling.</p>
15              <p class="boldText">This paragraph is being styled by the 'boldText' class selector.</p>
16              <p class="italicText">This paragraph is being styled by the 'italicText' class selector.</p>
17              <p class="underlinedText">And this paragraph is being styled by the 'underlinedText' class selector.</p>
18              <p>Now, we're back to a default-styled paragraph.</p>
19              <p class="boldText italicText">This paragraph is being targeted by two class selectors.</p>
20              <p class="italicText underlinedText">And this paragraph is being targeted by a different pair of selectors.</p>
21              <p class="boldText italicText underlinedText">Finally, this paragraph is targeted by all class selectors.</p>
22
23          </section>
24
25      </main>
26
```

```
 3  .boldText {
 4      font-weight: 700;
 5  }
 6
 7  .italicText {
 8      font-style: italic;
 9  }
10
11  .underlinedText {
12      text-decoration: underline;
13  }
14
```

```
file:///Volumes/Data/ACSound_loc  ×   +
file:///Volumes/Data/ACSound_local/Flame    C    Q Search

This paragraph is using default styling.

This paragraph is being styled by the 'boldText' class selector.

This paragraph is being styled by the 'italicText' class selector.

And this paragraph is being styled by the 'underlinedText' class selector.

Now, we're back to a default-styled paragraph.
```

Above: An element's class attribute can accept a list of class names; the style rules of all matching Class selectors will target the element.

But what if you want bold and italic text? Simple. Just list the class names in the element's class attribute, separating each class name with a space.

COMPOUND SELECTORS

Selectors can be combined in numerous ways, allowing us to become quite specific in the elements that we are targeting. Collectively these are known as compound selectors; let's take a look at a few of them.

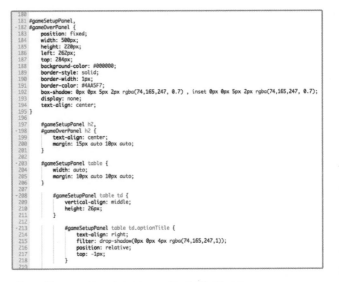

```
180
181  #gameSetupPanel,
182  #gameOverPanel {
183      position: fixed;
184      width: 500px;
185      height: 220px;
186      left: 262px;
187      top: 284px;
188      background-color: #000000;
189      border-style: solid;
190      border-width: 1px;
191      border-color: #4AA5F7;
192      box-shadow: 0px 0px 5px 2px rgba(74,165,247, 0.7) , inset 0px 0px 5px 2px rgba(74,165,247, 0.7);
193      display: none;
194      text-align: center;
195  }
196
197  #gameSetupPanel h2,
198  #gameOverPanel h2 {
199      text-align: center;
200      margin: 15px auto 10px auto;
201  }
202
203  #gameSetupPanel table {
204      width: auto;
205      margin: 10px auto 10px auto;
206  }
207
208      #gameSetupPanel table td {
209          vertical-align: middle;
210          height: 26px;
211      }
212
213          #gameSetupPanel table td.optionTitle {
214              text-align: right;
215              filter: drop-shadow(0px 0px 4px rgba(74,165,247,1));
216              position: relative;
217              top: -1px;
218          }
219
```

Above: We can combine selectors in a number of different ways.

Multiple Selectors

You may want to apply the same rule to a number of different elements or sets of elements. To do this we simply list the selectors we want to use, and separate each with a comma. For example:

```
h2, h3, p { style rule }
```

will target all <h2>, <h3> and <p> elements. We can take this a step further and include other compound selectors in the list of selectors, for example:

```
h2, h3, article.newsStory, p.newsStory { style rule }
```

Typed Class Selectors

We can take Class selectors a step further by combining them with a Type selector, for example:

```
article.newsStory { style rule }
```

This selector would target all <article> elements that had been given a classification of "newsStory"; an element such as <p class="newsStory"> would not receive the style rule because it is a <p> element, not an <article> element.

```
11          <main>
12              <section>
13
14                  <article class="newsStory">
15                      <p>This article has the 'newsStory' class applied to it.</p>
16                      <p>This class's style rule fills the element's background with a light grey color.</p>
17                      <p>Therefore, all of the paragraphs within the article are sitting on the article's grey background.</p>
18                  </article>
19
20                  <p class="newsStory">This paragraph is outside of the artice. It also has a 'newsStory' classification, but
     receives no styling.</p>
21
22              </section>
23
24          </main>
```

```
2
3 article.newsStory {
4     background-color: lightgrey;
5 }
6
```

Above: Typed Class selectors combine a Type and a Class selector.

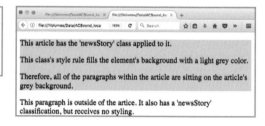

Descendant Selectors

There are times when we want to target an element based upon its position within the nested structure of the HTML. For example, we may want to target all <p> elements that are descended from (i.e. nested within, at any level) an <article> element (we touched on this back on page 50).

```
11          <main>
12              <section>
13
14                  <article>
15                      <p>These paragraphs are within an article element.</p>
16                      <p>A descendant selector is targeting them with a style rule that sets the text color to blue.</p>
17                      <div>
18                          <p>This paragraph is nested within a div element, which is itself nested within the article element. It
     still receives the descendant selector's styling</p>
19                      </div>
20                  </article>
21
22                  <p>This paragraph is not within an article element and so does not receive the descendant selector's styling.</p>
23
24              </section>
25
```

Above: Descendant selectors can target elements based on their position within the structure of the HTML.

Descendent selectors look like this (notice the space between the different names in the selector):

```
article p { style rule }
```

```
  2
▾ 3 article p {
  4      color: blue;
  5 }
  6
```

These paragraphs are within an article element.

A descendant selector is targeting them with a style rule that sets the text color to blue.

This paragraph is nested within a div element, which is itself nested within the article element. It still receives the descendant selector's styling

This paragraph is not within an article element and so does not receive the descendant selector's styling.

Above: Descendant selectors can target elements based on their position within the structure of the HTML.

Child Selectors

A Child selector targets elements that are children of another element (note that a Descendant selector also targets grandchildren, great grandchildren, etc.). A Child selector looks like this:

```
article > h3 { style rule }
```

This selector would target all <h3> elements that were direct children of an <article> element (notice the > between the different parts of the selector).

Pseudo-Class Selectors

A Pseudo-Class is a class that's not specifically declared in an HTML document, but that becomes

```
-11          <main>
-12              <section>
 13
▾14                  <article>
 15                      <h3>A Level-3 Heading</h3>
 16                      <p>The above heading is the direct child of an article element, and so is targeted by the Child selector.</p>
-17                      <div>
 18                          <h3>Another Level-3 Heading</h3>
 19                          <p>This second heading is within a div element which is itself nested within an article element. It did
    not recieve the style rule because it is not a direct child of the article element.</p>
 20                      </div>
 21                  </article>
 22                  <h3>Yet Another Level-3 Heading</h3>
 23                  <p>The third heading is not inside an article element at all, and so is not targeted by the Child selector.</p>
 24
 25              </section>
 26
 27          </main>
```

Above: Child selectors allow us to target elements that are the direct children of another targeted element.

A Level-3 Heading

The above heading is the direct child of an article element, and so is targeted by the Child selector.

Another Level-3 Heading

This second heading is within a div element which is itself nested within an article element. It did not recieve the style rule because it is not a direct child of the article element.

Yet Another Level-3 Heading

The third heading is not inside an article element at all, and so is not targeted by the Child selector.

available when the page is being viewed in a browser. For example, when the mouse pointer is over an element, the `hover` Pseudo-Class is assigned to that element.

```
 2
 3  article > h3 {
 4      color: purple;
 5  }
 6
```

Above: Child selectors allow us to target elements that are the direct children of another targeted element.

We target Pseudo-Classes using Pseudo-Class selectors, which look like this:

```
a:hover { style rule }
```

A selector is given, followed by a colon and then the name of a Pseudo-Class. In this example, the style rule would be applied to <a> elements when the mouse hovers over them.

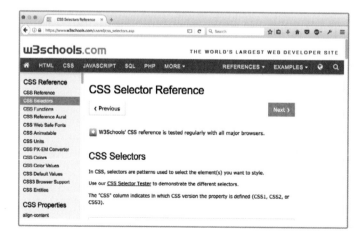

Above: The website www.w3schools.com has an excellent reference section that will help you to expand your coding knowledge.

A Massive Selection of Selectors

We don't have space in this book to list and explain the various forms of Pseudo-Class selectors, nor do we have space to cover some of the advanced forms of selector such as Structural Pseudo-Class selectors and Pseudo-Elements. When you feel ready to swot up on these, pop along to www.w3schools.com and look them up in the CSS reference section.

EXERCISE 8: USING SELECTORS

We've just found out about a whole load of different selectors, so to help lock in the information, we'll have a play around with some of them. We'll use the MyFirstWebPage project for this, and continue to improve on the page's appearance.

STARTING POINT

If you completed Exercise 5 (see page 83) then you can continue from where you left off. Alternatively, you can copy the files and folders from the downloadable code package's Exercise8\ startingPoint\ folder.

Hot Tip

The names used for ID and class selectors should start with a letter or an underscore, and should contain only letters, numbers and underscores: don't include spaces or any other symbol.

Name		Kind	Date Modified	Size
▼ 📁 css		Folder	15 Jun 2017, 12:13	--
	📄 MyFirstCSSDoc.css	Cascading Style Sheet File	15 Jun 2017, 12:07	32...ytes
▼ 📁 images		Folder	15 Jun 2017, 19:59	--
	🖼️ aboutImage.jpg	JPEG image	15 Jun 2017, 11:18	31 KB
▼ 📁 js		Folder	8 Jun 2017, 10:58	--
	📄 MyFirstJS.js	JavaScript file	8 Jun 2017, 11:01	48...ytes
📄 MyFirstWebPage.htm		HTML document	15 Jun 2017, 11:53	2 KB

MyFirstWebPage

Above: Your MyFirstWebPage project folder should look similar to this.

USING ID SELECTORS

1. Open MyFirstWebPage.htm in your code editor or IDE.

2. Locate the first <section> element (the one that contains the 'About' heading) and give it an id attribute with a value of "aboutSection".

```
22      <main>
23          <section id="aboutSection">
24              <h2>About</h2>
```

Above: Give the first <section> element an id of "aboutSection".

3. Locate the second <section> element (the one that contains the Blog heading) and give it an ID of "blogSection".

```
30          <section id="blogSection">
31              <h2>Blog</h2>
32              <article>
```

Above: Give the Blog section an ID of "blogSection".

4. Save the HTML document and then switch to (or open) MyFirstCSSDoc.css.

5. We're going to split the web page into two areas or panels; a left-hand area will show the About section, and a narrower right-hand area will show the Blog section. Now that we have set an id attribute for both <section> elements, we can target each with their own style rule.

6. Move to the bottom of the CSS document, create an empty line and type the selector #aboutSection (don't forget to also add the curly brackets to contain the style rule).

7. We're going to use the width style property to reduce the width of the About section (*see page 143 for more on sizing elements*). This property expects a length measurement as its value; a length can be written using various units, such as pixels (px), ems (em) and per cent (%); here, we're going to use per cent.

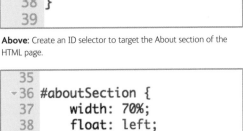

```
35
36 #aboutSection {
37
38 }
39
```

Above: Create an ID selector to target the About section of the HTML page.

8. Inside the #aboutSection style rule, add the following style properties and values:

```
width: 70%;
float: left;
```

```
35
36 #aboutSection {
37     width: 70%;
38     float: left;
39 }
40
```

Above: The #aboutSection style rule should look like this.

9. Add an ID selector for the `blogSection` element, and set its `width` property to 30% and its `float` property to `right`.

```
40
41 #blogSection {
42     width: 30%;
43     float: right;
44 }
45
```

Above: Yes, it's true, `float` works on more than just images!

10. Save your work and then open the web page in your browser.

Good Progress

Now we're getting somewhere! We've sized the two sections so that their widths add up to 100 per cent, and floated one to the left and the other to the right. We've been able to do this by using ID selectors to target style rules at each specific `<section>` element.

Left: Your page should now look something like this.

USING CLASS SELECTORS

1. Let's make the paragraph text in our Blog section look different to that in the About section. Open MyFirstWebPage.htm in your code editor/IDE and scroll down to the section element containing the Blog articles.

2. Add the `class` attribute to each `<p>` element within the Blog section, with an attribute value of `"blogText"`. Don't forget you can copy and paste the attribute and value to each `<p>`.

3. Save the HTML document and then open (or switch to) MyFirstCSSDoc. css. Scroll to the end of the document and create a couple of new lines to type into if needed.

```
30    <section id="blogSection">
31        <h2>Blog</h2>
32        <article>
33            <h3>Rockhopper says 'Thanks SpiderPenguin!'</h3>
34            <p class="blogText">A rockhopper had cause to say a big thank you to SpiderPe
35            <p class="blogText">'All seemed lost' said Rocky, but then in a flash of red
36        </article>
37
38        <article>
39            <h3>'Fish are tasty' says SpiderPenguin</h3>
40            <p class="blogText">It will come as no surprise to those who know him, but to
41        </article>
42
43    </section>
44
```

Above: The opening tags of the `<p>` elements in your Blog section should look like this.

4. We'll change the color of the text to help it look distinct (we look at CSS color on page 127). Add the following code to your CSS document:

```
.blogText {
    color: grey;
}
```

Hot Tip

When using CSS named colors (*see* page 127) we can use UK or US spellings of grey/gray.

5. Save your work and then open MyFirstWeb Page.htm in your browser. As you can see, the Class selector has changed the text color of all of the paragraphs whose `class` attribute was set to `"blogText"`.

```
46 .blogText {
47     color: grey;
48 }
```

Above: Add the `.blogText` class selector to your CSS document.

SpiderPenguin

The world's first fish-powered superhero

About

Following an accident involving kelp, toxic waste, a nuclear submarine and a tasty tuna fish, mild-mannered Peter Penguin was transformed into the one and only SpiderPenguin - the world's first fish-powered superhero. Orcas quake and leopard seals quiver when this penguin goes for a swim.

SpiderPenguin's powers include casting webs, climbing walls, and catching fish in the special spider-nets he fires from his super-flippers.

Faster than a torpedo, stronger than a whale, and cooler than a cucumber, SpiderPenguin always saves the day

Blog

Rockhopper says 'Thanks SpiderPenguin!'

A rockhopper had cause to say a big thank you to SpiderPenguin today: Whilst resting peacefully on a comfy iceberg, he was spotted by a pod of orcas who proceeded to take it in turns to try to wash him off the 'berg.

'All seemed lost' said Rocky, but then in a flash of red and blue, and a flurry of sticky web-like material, SpiderPenguin swooped in and plucked Rocky to safety. Phew-ee!

'Fish are tasty' says SpiderPenguin

It will come as no surprise to those who know him, but today SpiderPenguin shared with the world his thoughts on fish. 'Tasty' he said. Well - he is a penguin!

Above: All paragraphs classified as "blogText" have received the new Class selector's style rule.

DIFFERENT APPROACHES, SAME RESULTS

When writing CSS selectors, there's often more than one way to achieve the same visual result. In our previous step-by-step on class selectors, we used a Class selector to change the color of the paragraph text within blog articles, but we could also have used Descendant selectors.

USING DESCENDANT SELECTORS

1. Go back to your code editor/IDE and open the MyFirstWebPage.htm document. Delete all of the `class` attributes that you added in the previous exercise and then save the document.

2. Take a look at the nested structure of the Blog section's HTML. The `<p>` elements we wish to style are all contained within `<article>` elements, which themselves are all within an element that has an `id` of `"blogSection"`. We can use this structure to create a Descendant selector.

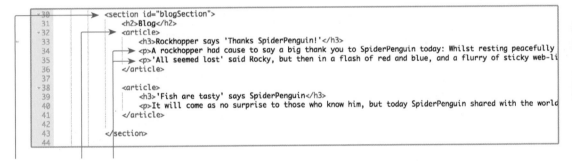

```
30    <section id="blogSection">
31        <h2>Blog</h2>
32        <article>
33            <h3>Rockhopper says 'Thanks SpiderPenguin!'</h3>
34            <p>A rockhopper had cause to say a big thank you to SpiderPenguin today: Whilst resting peacefully
35            <p>'All seemed lost' said Rocky, but then in a flash of red and blue, and a flurry of sticky web-li
36        </article>
37
38        <article>
39            <h3>'Fish are tasty' says SpiderPenguin</h3>
40            <p>It will come as no surprise to those who know him, but today SpiderPenguin shared with the world
41        </article>
42
43    </section>
44
```

`#blogSection article p { style rule }`   **Above:** Descendant selectors work with the nested structure of HTML elements.

3. Open MyFirstCSSDoc.css and locate the `.blogText` Class selector. Change the selector to the following:

    `#blogSection article p`

```
46 #blogSection article p {
47        color: grey;
48 }
```

Above: Replace the Class selector with a Descendant selector, but leave the style rule as it is.

4. Save your work and open the HTML file in your browser. The visual result is unchanged, but the grey-colored `<p>` elements are being targeted by a very different selector.

DEFINING AND APPLYING COLORS

An important part of any web design is the colors it uses. In CSS there are various ways of defining colors, and many style properties that can take a color as their value. Let's investigate.

COMPUTERS AND COLOR

Onscreen color is created by mixing together various amounts of red, green and blue light. For this reason, when designing for screen we define colors by specifying an amount of red, green and blue. On the web and in CSS each **color channel** - red, green or blue - can have a value between 0 and 255.

If all three values are 0 then you have black; if all three values are 255 you get white; if the red value is 255 and green and blue are both 0 you'll get pure red, and so on.

Hot Tip

Because in HTML and CSS the word color is spelled using the American English, we are also using this spelling throughout this book (the British English spelling would, of course, be colour).

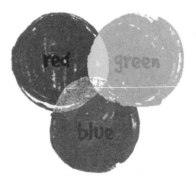
← RGB

Right: In computers colors are represented by different values for each of the color channels. RGB (red, green and blue) is relevant to us as it is used for defining colors in web pages.

COLOR IN CSS

There are a few different ways to define a color in CSS. The simplest, the one we used in the last exercise, is to use one of the predefined CSS color names. Just type the name of the color as the value of a color-based style property, and that's the color you'll get, for example:

Color Name	HEX	Color	Shades	Mix
AliceBlue	#F0F8FF		Shades	Mix
AntiqueWhite	#FAEBD7		Shades	Mix
Aqua	#00FFFF		Shades	Mix
Aquamarine	#7FFFD4		Shades	Mix
Azure	#F0FFFF		Shades	Mix
Beige	#F5F5DC		Shades	Mix
Bisque	#FFE4C4		Shades	Mix
Black	#000000		Shades	Mix
BlanchedAlmond	#FFEBCD		Shades	Mix
Blue	#0000FF		Shades	Mix
BlueViolet	#8A2BE2		Shades	Mix
Brown	#A52A2A		Shades	Mix
BurlyWood	#DEB887		Shades	Mix
CadetBlue	#5F9EA0		Shades	Mix

Above: You'll find a full listing of CSS' predefined colors at www.w3schools.com/cssref/css_colors.asp.

```
p.redText {
    color: red;
}
```

Specifying Exact Colors With `rgb()`

Whilst there are quite a few predefined colors in CSS, more often than not we will want to specify an exact color to use. One way to do this is to state the red, green and blue values of the color we wish to use, like this:

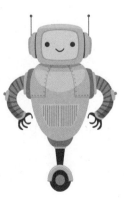

```
p.purpleText {
    color: rgb(102, 47, 172);
}
```

Specifying Exact Colors with Hexadecimal Values

Another way to specify colors in CSS is to use **hexadecimal**, or **hex** for short, color values. A hex color is written as a hash, #, followed by three pairs of hex numerals. The pairs of numerals represent the red, green and blue color values. For example this code:

```
p.purpleText {
    color: #662FAC;
}
```

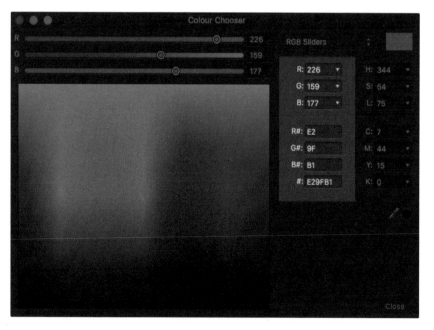

Above: Your image editor should be able to show you both RGB and hex color values.

would create the same color as the RGB color value used in the previous example. But how do we work out the hex values to put in there? The full answer to that question would require a maths lesson, but this isn't a maths book! There is a simpler way, though.

Looking up Hex Color Values

One way to look up a hex color value is with your graphics editor, which will almost certainly be able to display colors as hexadecimal values that you can copy and paste into your CSS. Alternatively, if you know the RGB values for a color then pop along to www.rgbtohex.net and use the page to convert to a hex color value.

Transparent Colors

Modern browsers support a third way of expressing color, one which allows us to specify how transparent (or see-through) the color will be.

It looks like this:

```
rgba(0, 255, 0, 0.5);
```

The red, green and blue channels are specified in the same way as they are when using `rgb()`. The fourth channel, a, is the **alpha** channel; it takes a value between 0, fully transparent, and 1, fully opaque.

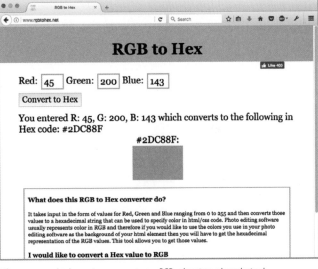

Above: www.rgbtohex.net can convert your RGB values into a hexadecimal color value.

Above: Using `rgba()` allows you to create semi-transparent colors through which background elements can be seen.

EXERCISE 9:
WORKING WITH COLORS

We've learned how colors work in CSS and HTML, so let's put that new knowledge into action by finding where those colors can be used.

COLOR ME GOOD

For this exercise, we'll continue to improve our MyFirstWebPage project by adding some more interesting colors. The colors you use on a page can make a dramatic difference, both to the page's legibility and to the overall mood and feel of the page.

Starting Point

If you've completed the previous exercises then you can continue to work from there; if you haven't completed those exercises then we've provided a starting point in the downloadable code package: Exercise9\startingPoint\MyFirstWebPage\.

Above: At the start of this exercise your project folder should look like this.

SETTING COLORS

Every visual element in HTML has a background-color style property. This, as you would expect, sets the color of the element's background (elements have transparent backgrounds by default). We're going to use some nice dark colors to give a smart overall appearance, but feel free to use your own colour values if you prefer.

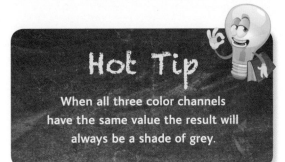

Hot Tip

When all three color channels have the same value the result will always be a shade of grey.

1. Setting the `<body>` element's `background-color` property will affect the entire page, so it's a good place to start. Open MyFirstCSSDoc. css in your code editor and find the

```
 1 body {
 2      font-family: "Arial", sans-serif;
 3      background-color: rgb(32, 32, 32);
 4 }
 5
```

```
41
42 #blogSection {
43      width: 30%;
44      float: right;
45      background-color: rgb(44, 56, 53);
46 }
47
```

Above: The body and the #blogSection style rules should now look like this.

body selector. Add the following to the selector's style rule:

```
background-color: rgb(32, 32, 32);
```

2. Let's also make the Blog section stand out by having a different background color. Locate the #blogSection selector and add the following to its style rule:

```
background-color: rgb(44, 56, 53);
```

3. Save your work and then open MyFirstWebPage.htm in your browser. The background colors look nice, but the text is now difficult to read; we need to make it lighter so that it contrasts more with the background color. We set text color using the `color` style property. If we set this property on the `<body>` element then it will cascade through the rest of the document.

4. Go back to your code editor and, in MyFirstCSSDoc.css, add the following to the `body` selector's style rule:

```
color: rgb(232, 232, 232);
```

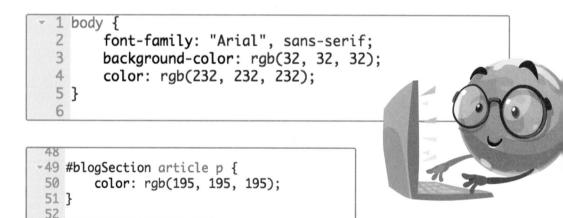

```
1 body {
2      font-family: "Arial", sans-serif;
3      background-color: rgb(32, 32, 32);
4      color: rgb(232, 232, 232);
5 }
6
```

```
48
49 #blogSection article p {
50     color: rgb(195, 195, 195);
51 }
52
```

Above: The body and `#blogSection article p` style rules should now look like this.

5. We also want the text color of Blog section articles to be a bit brighter than it is at present. Locate the `#blogSection article p` Descendant selector and, in its style rule, update the color property's value:

```
color: rgb(195, 195, 195);
```

6. Save the CSS document, return to your browser and refresh the page.

Spaced Out... or In

Things are starting to look good on our web page. As you can see, the text now stands out nicely against the background, but the text layout and positioning are not quite right; in some places, we need more space around text, in others we need less space. We've already had a brief look at the

Above: The `color` style property sets the foreground color of an element - for text-based elements the foreground color is the color the text will be drawn with.

`padding` style property (see page 89), but let's now look at how padding fits into the bigger picture of how CSS sizes and positions elements.

Hot Tip

When flipping back and forth between editor and web browser to see how code changes are affecting the page, hitting the browser's reload/refresh button will allow it to pick up and display the latest saved changes.

Above: We're getting there, but the text layout is still not right, and we need to fix that.

THE CSS BOX MODEL

When rendered by a web browser, every visual element creates a box in which its content is drawn. We can control the size, position and behaviour of that box with CSS.

THE ELEMENT BOX

At the heart of the web page layout is the **element box**. Every element produces one and, with the exception of some table elements, every element's box has the same basic features.

Above: Web browsers render every element inside its own onscreen box.

Inner Content Area

At the centre of the element box is the inner content area that contains the actual visual content of the element: text, an image, a video or whatever. When we set an element's size or position, it is the inner content area that is being sized or positioned.

Padding

Padding is optional empty space that surrounds the inner content area. We can specify padding on a per-side basis, or apply the same padding value to every side of the box.

Border Box

Surrounding the inner content and padding areas is the border box. The edges of the border box can be made visible, creating an outline around the element's content and padding. The width, color and style of that outline can also be set via style properties. All of the style properties controlling the border appearance can be set per side, or for all sides at once.

Hot Tip

Margins lie outside of the background area of their element and so, unlike padding, never show the element's background color or image; in other words, margins are always transparent.

Margins

Finally, on the outside of the border box are the element's margins. These create space between the element and the other elements around it; in other words, the elements that are **adjacent** to it.

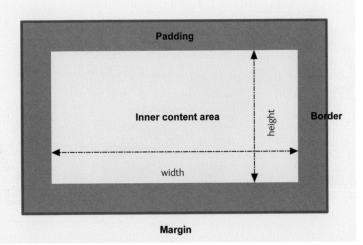

Right Model of the CSS element box.

Margin Overlaps

The margins of adjacent elements aren't added together; rather, they overlap each other. In effect, this means that the gap between two adjacent elements is determined by the element that has the largest margin on the adjacent side.

For example, imagine we have two images, `image1` and `image2`, that are side by side on the page, with `image1` to the left of `image2`. `image1`'s `margin-right` property is set to `10px` whilst `image2`'s `margin-left` property is set to `15px`.

In this situation it is `image2` that has the larger adjacent margin, and so the gap between the two elements will be `15px`.

Above: Margins overlap each other, and it's the larger margin that determines the gap between adjacent elements.

EXERCISE 10: WORKING WITH PADDING AND MARGINS

Our MyFirstWebPage project is showing some promise, but the text layout needs some improvement. We can sort this out by playing around with element box style properties.

STARTING POINT

If you've completed the previous exercises then carry on from where you left off, otherwise you can copy our starting point from 'Exercise10\startingPoint\' in the downloadable code package.

SETTING MARGINS AND PADDING

1. Let's start by looking at the main page heading, where the gap between the heading and subheading (within the <hgroup>, as you will recall) is a bit large. This gap is being introduced by the default margins being applied to the <h1> and <h2> elements.

Above: Once again, we've provided starting point code for this exercise, or you can continue with your own MyFirstWebPage project.

2. Open MyFirstCSSDoc.css in your code editor, move to the end of the document and create a new line. We want to target the rule at all <h1> and <h2> elements that are within an <hgroup> element, so add the following selector to the document:

```
hgroup > h1, hgroup > h2
```

```
 15        <header>
 16            <hgroup>
 17                <h1>SpiderPenguin</h1>
 18                <h2>The world's first fish-powered superhero</h2>
 19            </hgroup>
 20        </header>
 21
```

Above: <h1> and <h2> are both children of the <hgroup> element, and so both headings will be targeted by the multiple child selectors.

3. If we want the same margin to be applied to all sides of an element we can write something like this:

```
margin: 10px;
```

However, in this instance we want to set the top and bottom margins, whilst leaving the left and right margins at 0px (which is what they are by default). One way to do this is by using the margin-top and margin-bottom style properties; add the following to your new style rule:

```
 52
 53 hgroup > h1, hgroup > h2 {
 54     margin-top: 2px;
 55     margin-bottom: 2px;
 56 }
 57
```

```
margin-top: 2px;
margin-bottom:2px;
```

Above: The new selector and style rule should look like this.

4. Save your work and then open MyFirstWebPage.htm in your web browser. As you can see, the gap is now much nicer, but the pair of headings has now moved closer to the top of the page, and the main page content has moved up towards the heading also. We can fix this by padding the `<header>` element.

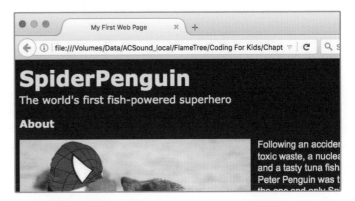

5. Flip back to MyFirstCSSDoc.css in your code editor. On a new line, add the following Type selector and style rule:

```
header {

    padding-top:10px;
    padding-bottom:10px;
}
```

Above: The `<hgroup>` headings have closed up nicely, but now things are just a little cramped at the top of the page.

6. Save the CSS document, flip back to your web browser and reload the page. We've added space *inside* the `<header>` element using padding. This has pushed the `<header>` element's content, the `<hgroup>`, down the page, and opened more of a gap between the `<hgroup>` and `<main>` areas of the page; in short, it looks good!

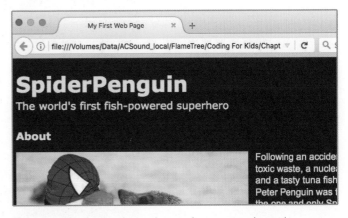

Above: By padding the `<header>`, we've opened up some space above and below the `<hgroup>` headings.

7. Let's now tackle the vertical gap between the text in the About section and the text in the Blog section. You may think the easiest way of doing this is to add some padding to the two `<section>` elements; let's see what happens if you do this.

8. Locate the `#aboutSection` selector and add this to its style rule:

   `padding-right: 10px;`

   Then locate the `#blogSection` selector and add this:

   `padding-left: 10px;`

```
37
38 #aboutSection {
39     width: 70%;
40     float: left;
41     padding-right: 10px;
42 }
43
44 #blogSection {
45     width: 30%;
46     float: right;
47     background-color: rgb(44, 56, 53);
48     padding-left: 10px;
49 }
50
```

Above: You may think that padding the `<section>` elements will do the trick.

9. Save the document, switch over to your browser and reload the page. Oh dear, that didn't work! The problem is that we have already set the `width` of the two `<section>` elements so that they added up to 100 per cent (the width of the page); by then adding padding, we have made the elements wider than the page, and so the second has had to wrap to a new line.

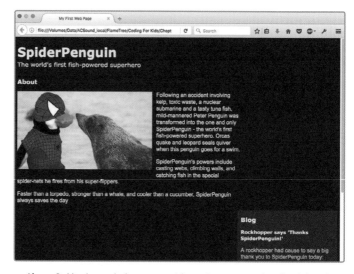

Above: Padding has made the two `<section>` elements too wide to fit side by side!

10. Return to the CSS document and undo the changes you made in step 8. What we need to do instead is set margins on the children of the `<section>` elements.

11. In the About section it's only the right-hand edges of `<p>` elements that extend as far as the Blog section's text, and we can target these elements with a simple Descendant selector that will target all of the `<p>` elements within `<section id="aboutSection">`.

12. Add the following to your CSS document:

```
#aboutSection p {
    margin-right: 10px;
}
```

Hot Tip

Padding and margins can have similar visual outcomes, so it's not always obvious which is best to use in a given situation. Adding background colors whilst experimenting can help to reveal the answer.

```
42
43  #aboutSection p {
44      margin-right: 10px;
45  }
46
```

Above: Use a Descendant selector to target all `<p>` elements that are within `<section id="aboutSection">`.

13. We need to set both left and right margins for the Blog section, and we need to set these margins on more than one type of element. If you study the section's HTML

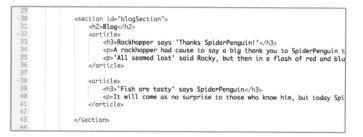

```
29
30   <section id="blogSection">
31       <h2>Blog</h2>
32       <article>
33           <h3>Rockhopper says 'Thanks SpiderPenguin!'</h3>
34           <p>A rockhopper had cause to say a big thank you to SpiderPenguin t
35           <p>'All seemed lost' said Rocky, but then in a flash of red and blu
36       </article>
37
38       <article>
39           <h3>'Fish are tasty' says SpiderPenguin</h3>
40           <p>It will come as no surprise to those who know him, but today Spi
41       </article>
42
43   </section>
44
```

Above: The HTML reveals that the `<section id="blogSection">` element has two types of child element: `<h2>` and `<article>`.

code you should see that the direct children of `<section id="blogSection">` are `<h2>` and `<article>` elements.

14. Add the following selector and style rule to your CSS document:

```
#blogSection > h2, #blogSection > article {
    margin-left: 10px;
    margin-right: 10px;
}
```

15. Save your work, flip over to your web browser and reload the page. Success! By using margins and padding we've made things look much neater and more attractive. Go ahead and play around with margins and padding on the other elements and see if you can make things look better still.

Above: Adjusting the padding and margins has made the page look much better.

SIZING

Sizing an element is not as simple as setting its width and height style properties; many other factors have to be thought about too.

THE DISPLAY STYLE PROPERTY

When a web browser lays out a page, each element is generated in the same order as it appears in the HTML document. The display style property plays a part in controlling how each element box is laid out, and how much space it will occupy within the layout.

Block Elements

An element whose display style property has been set to block is referred to as a **block** or **block-level** element. Under normal circumstances, a block-level element creates a new line in its containing element's layout and will fill the width of that containing element, causing any following elements to be drawn below it. `<main>`, `<div>` and `<p>` are all examples of elements that are usually block-level.

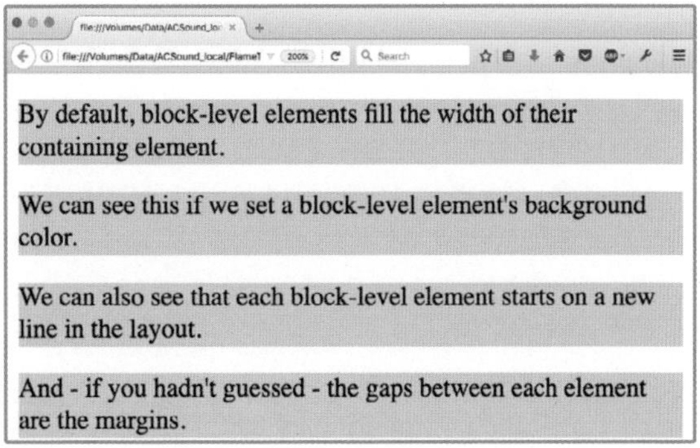

```
 9    <body>
10
11        <p>By default, block-level elements fill the width of their containing element.</p>
12        <p>We can see this if we set a block-level element's background color.</p>
13        <p>We can also see that each block-level element starts on a new line in the layout.</p>
14        <p>And - if you hadn't guessed - the gaps between each element are the margins.</p>
15
16    </body>
17
```

Above: Setting the background-color style property on these `<p>` elements shows how block-level elements are laid out.

Inline Elements

An element whose display property has been set to inline is known as an **inline** element. Inline elements don't create a new line in the containing element's layout, and only occupy the space they need. `<img>`, `<a>` and `<span>` are examples of inline elements.

Hot Tip

Using display: none; is a good method of hiding an element - it still exists *in* the page, but isn't drawn *on* the page.

Invisible Elements

An element whose display property is none is left out of the page layout altogether. The element does still exist in the document, it just isn't rendered on the page.

Value	Description	Play it
inline	Default value. Displays an element as an inline element (like <span>)	Play it »
block	Displays an element as a block element (like <p>)	Play it »
flex	Displays an element as a block-level flex container. New in CSS3	
inline-block	Displays an element as an inline-level block container. The inside of this block is formatted as block-level box, and the element itself is formatted as an inline-level box	
inline-flex	Displays an element as an inline-level flex container. New in CSS3	
inline-table	The element is displayed as an inline-level table	
list-item	Let the element behave like a <li> element	Play it »
run-in	Displays an element as either block or inline, depending on context	
table	Let the element behave like a <table> element	
table-caption	Let the element behave like a <caption> element	
table-column-group	Let the element behave like a <colgroup> element	
table-header-group	Let the element behave like a <thead> element	

Other Values for Display

There are quite a few other values for display, and these are mainly used by tables and lists. If you want to see a full list of values then visit www.w3schools.com and look up the display property in the site's CSS reference section.

Left: Reference sites such as www. w3schools.com will give a full list of the different values for display.

THE CONTAINING ELEMENT

We've mentioned the containing element a number of times over the last couple of pages and you may think this is another way of referring to an element's parent element, but there's slightly more to it. When it comes to page layout, an element's containing element is the nearest block-level parent.

SETTING SIZE PROPERTIES

We can specify the size of an element using the `width` and `height` style properties, but these properties only control the inner content area (*see* page 134): the `padding`, `border-width` and `margin` values also play their part in determining the actual size of an element's box.

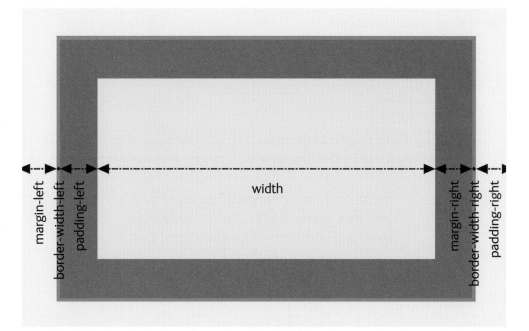

Above: All parts of the element box add up to give the overall width of the box.

Auto Sizing

All of the CSS box model style properties, `margin`, `padding`, `width`, and so on, can be given a value of `auto`, instructing the browser to calculate the value that should be used.

> ## Hot Tip
>
> Most elements use a default value of `auto` for their `width` and `height` style properties.

The `auto` value is useful because it allows us to control the size and position of an element via different style properties. For example, if a `<p>` element's `width` property is `auto`, and if we increase its `padding` property, the `width` of the element will reduce in order to accommodate the increased padding value, whilst remaining within its containing element. And if by reducing the `width` of the `<p>` the text is forced to wrap on to a new line, then having a `height` value of `auto` ensures that the element box will resize too.

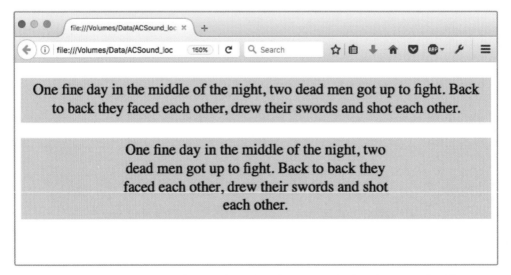

Above: Notice how the `width` and `height` of the second `<p>` element have automatically adjusted to accommodate different `padding-left` and `padding-right` values.

POSITIONING

One of the fiddliest areas of CSS is positioning. There are four style properties that you can use to set an element's offset position, but how, and indeed if, they work depends on the four positioning modes.

OFFSET STYLE PROPERTIES

The four style properties that can be used for setting an element's offset position are left, right, top and bottom. They take any measurement unit as their value, pixels, per cent and so on, or can have their value set to auto.

POSITIONING MODES

An element's positioning mode controls how the offset properties affect the element. The mode is set using the position style property; let's look at its four possible values: static, relative, absolute and fixed.

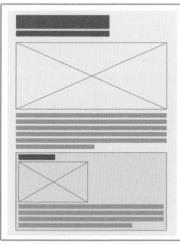

Above: Static positioned elements are laid out one after another, according to where they appear in the HTML.

Static Positioning

The element occupies its normal place in the layout flow of the document. The offset properties have no effect on the element. Static positioning is the default for all elements.

Relative Positioning

The element is offset by some way from the location it would normally occupy in the layout flow of the document. The offset style properties control how far the element is offset from its normal location. For example, left: 8px; would move the element eight pixels to the left of its normal position. The space the element would have occupied remains in the document layout and is not closed up.

Absolute Positioning

The element is removed from the flow of the document layout and positioned relative to its nearest non-static containing element.

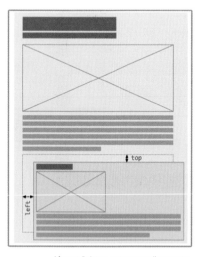

Above: Relative positioning allows us to offset an element from where it would have appeared if statically positioned.

Above: Absolute positioned elements are removed from the layout flow and offset relative to their containing block.

The offset style properties determine the location of the element relative to this containing element. For example, `top: 20px;` would move the element so that its top edge lay 20 pixels below the containing element's top edge. The space the element would have occupied in the document is closed up.

Fixed Positioning

The element is removed from the flow of the document layout and positioned relative to the browser window. The offset style properties determine the position of the element inside the browser window. For example, `bottom: 150px;` would place the element so that its bottom edge was 150 pixels above the browser window's bottom edge. The space the element would have occupied in the document is closed up.

Above: Fixed positioned elements are removed from the layout flow and placed relative to the browser window.

OVERSIZED BOXES

With all of the different properties that affect it, it's not uncommon to end up setting those properties in such a way as to force an element box to be larger than its containing element; what happens then?

OVERFLOW

When an element's box is sized or positioned outside of its containing element's box, the value of the overflow style property comes into play. This determines what should happen with the parts of the element that are overspilling the container.

Values for the Overflow Property

- ▸ **visible**
  The overspilling content is not clipped and is shown.

- ▸ **hidden**
  The overspilling content is clipped and is not shown.

- ▸ **scroll**
  The overspilling content is not shown, but scroll bars are drawn so that it can be accessed.

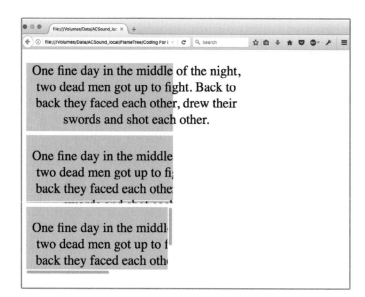

Above: The outcome of the three different **overflow** values.

Direction-Specific Overflow

As well as the single overflow style property, we can control the horizontal and vertical overflow separately: overflow-x controls the horizontal overspill, whilst overflow-y controls the vertical overspill.

PUTTING SIZING AND POSITIONING INTO PRACTICE

We'll be using the sizing and positioning style properties quite a lot in Chapter 5: Playing With Code (see page 198), so we aren't going to do any practical exercises with them at present. For now, park the information in a convenient portion of your brain, and then strap in and hold on tight because it's time to take a ride through the wonderful world of JavaScript.

```
207
208    #gameSetupPanel table td {
209        vertical-align: middle;
210        height: 26px;
211    }
212
213    #gameSetupPanel table td.optionTitle {
214        text-align: right;
215        filter: drop-shadow(0px 0px 4px rgba(74,165,247,1));
216        position: relative;
217        top: -1px;
218    }
219
220    #gameSetupPanel table select {
221        width: 60px;
222        margin: 5px 10px 5px 10px;
223    }
224
225    #gameSetupPanel button,
226    #gameOverPanel button {
227        width: auto;
228        height: 24px;
229        margin: 10px 10px 10px 10px;
230        padding: 0px 20px 1px 20px;
231    }
232
```

Above: We'll be coming back to sizing and positioning in Chapter 5.

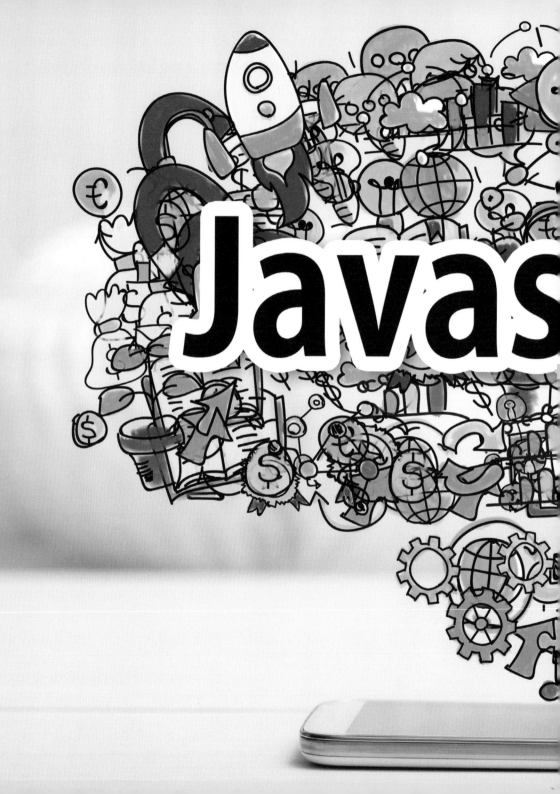

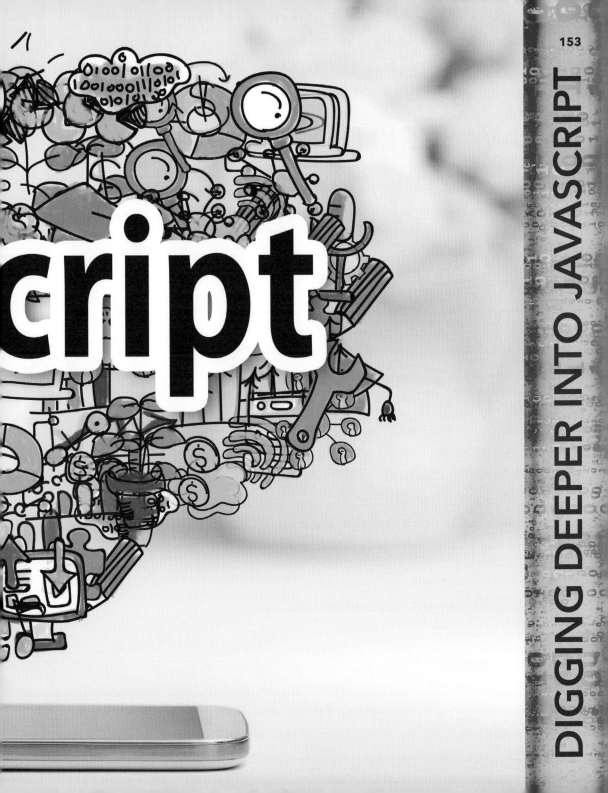

cript

JAVASCRIPT SYNTAX

A script can consist of a single instruction or be a vast document containing thousands of lines of code. No matter the size though, all JavaScript scripts share a common structure and syntax.

CASE-SENSITIVITY

JavaScript is case-sensitive. In other words lower-case letters are seen as different to the upper-case version of the same letter. For example, `myValue` is not the same as `MyValue` (notice the different capitalizations).

WHITESPACE

Spaces and tabs are ignored in JavaScript. This allows us to use code indenting, just like in HTML (*see page 31*), and it serves the same purpose of making the code better organized and easier to read.

```
65
66 com.flametreepublishing.cfk.CodeBreakerGame.prototype.getNextSymbolId = function(aSymbolId) {
67     var theResult;
68     for (var i = 0; i < this.codeSymbolIds.length; i++) {
69         if (this.codeSymbolIds[i] == aSymbolId) {
70             if (i == this.codeSymbolIds.length -1) {
71                 theResult = this.codeSymbolIds[0];
72             } else {
73                 theResult = this.codeSymbolIds[(i+1)];
74             }
75             break;
76         }
77     }
78     return(theResult);
79 }
80
```

Above: Indented code is quite easy to read because it helps to visualize the structure and flow of your code.

SEMICOLONS

JavaScript **statements** normally end with a semicolon, but this isn't a strict rule. If you leave out a semicolon, the interpreter (see page 53) will assume line-breaks mark the end of a statement. However, leaving out semicolons can make your code confusing and lead to mistakes, so you should be sure to end every statement with a semicolon.

COMMENTS

A **comment** is a section of script that will be ignored by the interpreter. Comments are used for adding notes and explanations to scripts, helping others to understand them, and acting as notes-to-self if you revisit a script you wrote months earlier.

Inline Comments

An inline comment starts with / / and continues until the next line break. It can be placed on a line following other JavaScript code.

```
3
4  //Inline comments start with '//' and end at the next line break
5
6  var userScore = 0; //They can be written on the same line as other code
7
8  //They can also be used to disable lines of code, for example...:
9  //window.alert(userScore);
10
11
```

Above: Inline comments end at the line break that follows the comment.

Block Comments

A block comment starts with / * and continues until a closing * / occurs. Everything between these markers is considered part of the comment.

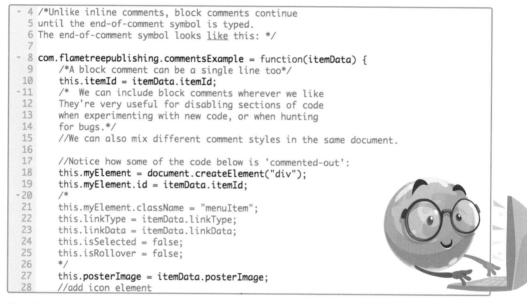

```
 4  /*Unlike inline comments, block comments continue
 5  until the end-of-comment symbol is typed.
 6  The end-of-comment symbol looks like this: */
 7
 8  com.flametreepublishing.commentsExample = function(itemData) {
 9       /*A block comment can be a single line too*/
10       this.itemId = itemData.itemId;
11       /*  We can include block comments wherever we like
12       They're very useful for disabling sections of code
13       when experimenting with new code, or when hunting
14       for bugs.*/
15       //We can also mix different comment styles in the same document.
16
17       //Notice how some of the code below is 'commented-out':
18       this.myElement = document.createElement("div");
19       this.myElement.id = itemData.itemId;
20       /*
21       this.myElement.className = "menuItem";
22       this.linkType = itemData.linkType;
23       this.linkData = itemData.linkData;
24       this.isSelected = false;
25       this.isRollover = false;
26       */
27       this.posterImage = itemData.posterImage;
28       //add icon element
```

Above: Block comments can extend across multiple lines.

IDENTIFIERS

An **identifier** is a name that's given, or **assigned**, to a piece of data (*see* page 158) or to a function (*see* page 188). Once assigned, an identifier can be used to refer to that data (or function) within a script. JavaScript leaves you free to choose the names you wish to use as identifiers, so long as you follow a few basic rules:

Hot Tip

Comments are commonly used to disable sections of a script, very useful when experimenting with new ideas or attempting to hunt down bugs.

Identifier Naming Rules

○ **Reserved words:** JavaScript defines a number of words that have special meaning for the language (*see below*). These can't be used as names for your own identifiers.

○ **First character:** The first character of an identifier must be a letter, an underscore _ or a dollar $.

○ **Other characters:** The remaining characters in an identifier can only be letters, numbers, underscores or dollars.

```
 3  //Examples of legal identifiers
 4  myValue
 5  _myValue
 6  MY_VALUE
 7  $myvalue
 8  my$Value23
 9  my_$_value_23
10
11  //Examples of illegal identifiers
12  23myvalue
13  myValue*
14  my-value
15  #myvalue
16  my%value
17  my¢Value
```

Above: The first set of identifiers are all legal (i.e. allowed) identifiers, the second set are illegal.

Keywords and Other Reserved Words

JavaScript has a set of predefined identifiers, called **keywords**, as well as other identifiers that may be added to the language in the future. Taken together these are known as **reserved words**, and you mustn't use these as names for your own identifiers (nor as property names within objects, *see* page 168).

Below: JavaScript's reserved words; don't use these for your own identifier names.

KEYWORDS

break, case, catch, continue, default, delete, do, else, false, finally, for, function, if, in, instanceof, new, null, return, switch, this, throw, true, try, typeof, var, void, while, with

OTHER RESERVED WORDS

abstract, boolean, byte, char, class, const, debugger, double, enum, export, extends, final, float, goto, implements, import, int, interface, long, native, package, private, protected, public, short, static, super, synchronized, throws, transient, volatile

DATA AND VARIABLES

An important concept in all programming languages is data. Data can be thought of as any piece of information that's used within a program.

ALL DATA HAS A VALUE

Any piece of data can be said to have a **value**. This value can be simple: for example, a number or a paragraph of text; or it can be complex, such as a list of numbers or paragraphs. Whatever the type of data though, the information being represented by that data is referred to as the data's value.

Below: Literal values are typed directly into a script.

```
3
4 myNumberLiteral = 42;
5 myStringLiteral = "Hello World";
6 myBooleanLiteral = true;
7 myNullLiteral = null;
8
```

Literals

A **literal** is a piece of data with a specific value that's typed directly into a script. The following are all examples of literals:

`"Hello World"`, `true`, `42`, `null`.

EXERCISE 11: **USING VARIABLES**

In essence, a variable is a portion of computer memory that's used for storing data, and which is referred to using an identifier.

DECLARING A VARIABLE

It's very easy to write, or **declare**, a new variable in JavaScript: all we do is write the keyword `var` followed by the identifier we want to use to refer to the variable. For example:

```
var theAnswer;
```

Assigning a Value to a Variable

It's common to assign a value to a variable at the time it's declared, like this:

```
var theAnswer = 42;
```

Changing the Value of a Variable

Once a variable has been declared with `var` we can change the value assigned to it like this:

Hot Tip

In JavaScript = does not mean 'equals', it means 'assignment' (*see* page 177).

`theAnswer = 54`. Notice that we didn't include the `var` keyword this time.

Below: Variables are easy to declare and use.

```
3
4  //Declaring variables (without and with assignment)
5  var theQuestion;
6  var theAnswer = 42;
7
8  //Assigning a value to a declared variable
9  theQuestion = "Life, the Universe and Everything";
10
```

GETTING THE VALUE OF A VARIABLE

1. To use the value stored in a variable, we write that variable's identifier name in the place where we need to use the value.

2. Create a new HTML document and add the required structural elements (`<html>`, `<head>` and `<body>`). Save the document as gettingVariables.htm.

3. Add a `<script type= "text/javascript">` element as a child of (in other words, within) the `<body>` element.

```
 1  <!DOCTYPE HTML>
 2
 3  <html>
 4
 5      <head>
 6
 7      </head>
 8
 9      <body>
10
11          <script type="text/javascript">
12
13          </script>
14
15      </body>
16
17  </html>
18
```

Above: The basic structural elements of an HTML document.

4. Add the JavaScript code shown below.

Below: Copy this script into your document.

```
10
11          <script type="text/javascript">
12              var theMessage = "The alert function displays a message in a dialog box.";
13              window.alert(theMessage);
14              theMessage = "Here we're just changing a variable's value...";
15              window.alert(theMessage);
16              theMessage = "...and passing that variable's identifier to the alert function.";
17              window.alert(theMessage);
18              theMessage = "The interpreter then looks up the variable's value...";
19              window.alert(theMessage);
20              theMessage = "...and that's what we see in the dialog box. Simple, eh?";
21              window.alert(theMessage);
22          </script>
23
```

5. Save your work and then open the file in your web browser.

DATATYPES

All data handled by JavaScript has a datatype. This specifies the nature of the data being handled, whether it's a number, text, a list, and so on.

WHAT IS A DATATYPE?

In order to be able to use a piece of data, a computer or program has to know what the data represents - in other words, it has to know the datatype of the data. Because data is stored in variables, we normally refer to variables as having a datatype, or as being of type so-and-so. Datatypes fall into two groups: primitive and reference. Let's take a look at what that means.

Above: Datatypes give meaning to the raw numbers stored in the computer's memory.

PRIMITIVE AND REFERENCE DATATYPES

Primitive datatypes can be thought of as those whose data represents a single value, such as a number, whilst **reference** datatypes represent complex data, such as a list. When a variable of a primitive type is used in a script, the interpreter copies the variable's value and uses this copy in its calculations. In contrast, when a variable of reference type is used, the interpreter works directly with the data stored in memory; any changes to the variable's value will affect anything else that uses that variable.

THE PRIMITIVE DATATYPES

Let's take a look at the primitive datatypes. Remember, variables of these types represent a single, simple value.

Primitive data type

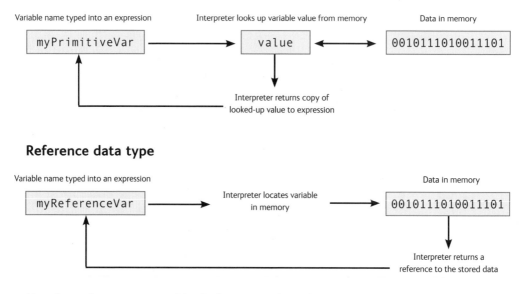

Above: Primitive datatypes return a copy of their data from memory; reference datatypes return the actual data stored in memory.

Booleans

Booleans are the simplest datatype there is. A Boolean can have a value of either `false` or `true`. These values are actually represented within the computer as 0 or 1 (respectively) and you can in fact use those numbers in place of `false` and `true`.

Numbers

Generally, in computing, there are two types of number: integers and floats. Integers are whole numbers; floats are fractions, such as 3.14, or scientific numbers called exponential numbers, which look like this: $0.945x10^7$. JavaScript doesn't worry itself with such distinctions: a number is a number.

Strings

Strings are text data. Don't worry about why they're called strings (it gets technical in ways we don't need to worry about); just know that a string is text, and text is a string.

When writing strings into scripts, they have to be surrounded by quote marks. These can be single ' or double " quotes, but a string must be closed by the same style of quote mark that it was opened with.

We often need to create an empty string; in other words a string with no actual text in it. To do this we write a pair of quote marks: ' ' or " ".

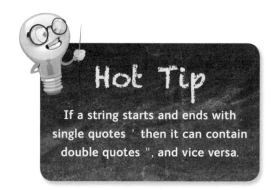

Hot Tip

If a string starts and ends with single quotes ' then it can contain double quotes ", and vice versa.

```
8
9    <script type="text/javascript">
10
11        var anyString = ""; //"" creates an empty string
12        anyString = 'A string can be demarked by single quotes...';
13        anyString = "...or it can be demarked by double quotes.";
14        anyString = 'A string demarked by single quotes "can" contain double quotes';
15        anyString = "A string demarked by double quotes 'can' contain single quotes";
16
17    </script>
18
```

Above: Different ways of using quote marks with strings.

The null Type

null indicates that there is no value; if a variable has a datatype of null then it doesn't contain any valid data or, most likely, has not even been declared.

The undefined Type

undefined is slightly different to null: it is the initial datatype (and value) of any variable that has been declared but not yet had a value, and therefore a datatype, assigned to it.

THE REFERENCE DATATYPES

As already mentioned, when working with a variable of a reference datatype, you are actually working directly with the data that's stored in memory; any changes to the data will affect anything that uses that same variable.

```
10
11      <script type="text/javascript">
12
13          //Note: The typeof operator tells us the datatype of a variable
14          var myVar;
15          window.alert(typeof myVar); //shows 'undefined'
16          myVar = "Hello World";
17          window.alert(typeof myVar); //shows 'string'
18
19      </script>
20
```

Above: In this example, the datatype of myVar is undefined until it is assigned a value (why not try this script yourself?).

ARRAYS

An array is simply a list of values. The values in the array can be of any datatype. We work with an array in a number of different ways: adding or removing values, or simply reading the values within the array.

Creating an Array

We create an array in a couple of ways. The first is to write, or declare, an array literal, like this:

```
var namesList = ["Oliver", "Kate", "Sajid", "Harry", "Monisha"];
```

The square brackets mark the start and end of the array, whilst each value of the array is separated with a comma. The other way to create an array is using the new keyword:

```
var myArray = new Array();
```

Initial values for the array can be included within the brackets if required.

```
 9    <script type="text/javascript">
10
11        var emptyArray = [];
12        var numbersArray = [42, 12, 57, 3.14, 901582, 5];
13        var stringsArray = ["Oliver", "Kate", "Sajid", "Harry", "Monisha"];
14        var mixedArray = ["Oliver", true, false, 5]
15        var arraysArray = [emptyArray, numbersArray, stringsArray, mixedArray];
16
17    </script>
```

Above: Arrays store lists of other data (including other arrays).

Accessing the Values in an Array

Each piece of data stored in an array is referred to as an element of the array. Each element has an `index`, this being a number that's the position of the element within the array. The first element has an index of 0, the second an index of 1 and so on. To access a specific element of an array then, we type the array variable's name followed by the index number wrapped in square brackets. For example, if we want to use the third element (index 2) of the array `myArray` we write `myArray[2]`.

Other Array Methods

Arrays have many other **methods** that we use to manipulate their content (*see* page 194, for more about methods). However, if you want to discover more about them then do a web search for JavaScript array methods.

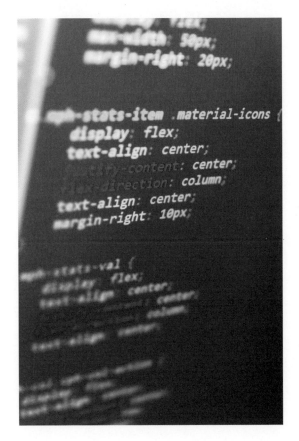

```
 8
 9    <script type="text/javascript">
10
11        var namesArray = ["Oliver", "Kate", "Sajid", "Harry", "Monisha"];
12        window.alert(namesArray[2]); //Will show 'Sajid' in the alert popup
13        window.alert(namesArray.length) //Will show '5' in the alert popup
14        namesArray.push("Kristoff"); //Adds "Kristoff" to the array
15        window.alert(namesArray.length) //Will now show '6' in the alert popup
16
```

Above: Arrays have a number of properties and methods; here we're using the `length` property and `push()` method.

OBJECTS

A variable of type object is a variable in which we can store multiple values but, unlike an array, where each element is accessed via its position within the array, an object stores values against named **properties** (often called a property-value pair).

> ## Hot Tip
>
> The values stored in the properties of an object can be of any datatype, including arrays or other objects.

Objects play a special role in JavaScript. They are the basic building block upon which all other JavaScript data is built. Every other datatype inherits its basic characteristics from Object. For this reason we often (and from now on will) refer to any and all JavaScript data as being an object: a string object, for example, an array object, or, indeed, an object object.

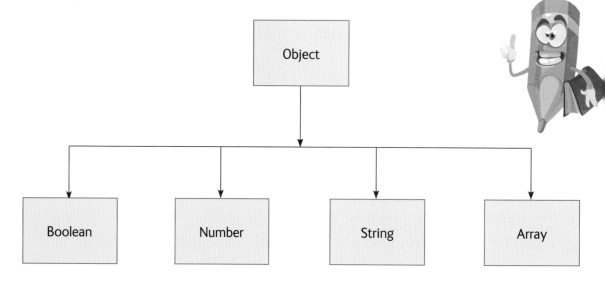

Above: All JavaScript objects are built on the object datatype.

EXERCISE 12:
CREATING OBJECTS

Objects are fundamental to JavaScript, and so it's very important to understand them and be comfortable working with them.

CREATING A NEW OBJECT

1. We can create an object either by typing an object literal or by using the new keyword. Let's try both. Create a new HTML document containing the standard structural elements (<html>, <head> and <body>) and save it as javascriptObjects.htm. Within the <body> element, add the following:

    ```
    <script type="text/javascript">
    ```

    ```
    10
    11      <script type="text/javascript">
    12
    13          var player1 = new Object();
    14          player1.name = "Cathy";
    15          player1.age = 15;
    16          player1.maxScore = 40562634;
    17
    18      </script>
    19
    ```

    Above: Figure 12-1: Enter this JavaScript code into your document.

2. Enter the JavaScript code shown in Figure 12-1, above. This uses the new keyword to create an empty object, then declares a number of properties on that object.

3. Add the code shown in Figure 12-2, below. This creates an object by declaring an object literal. Within the object literal, each property name is followed by a colon and a value, and property-value pairs are separated by commas. The whole literal is wrapped in **braces** (i.e. curly brackets, { }).

```
17
18          var player2 = {name: "Tula", age: 14, maxScore: 25693725};
19
```

Above: Figure 12-2: Add this object literal to your script.

4. Add the code shown in Figure 12-3. This declares another object literal, but this time it's an empty one that could be used for storing information generated as the page runs.

```
19
20          var currentGameScores = {};
21
```

Above: Figure 12-3: Finally, declare a new, empty object with this object literal.

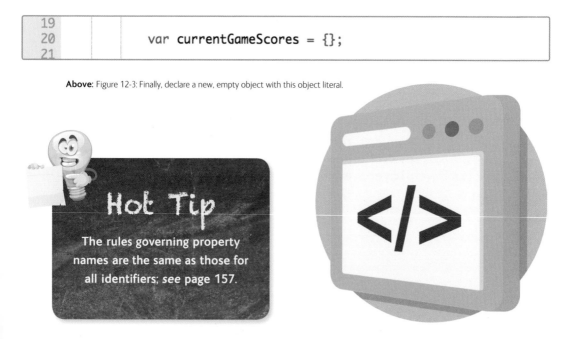

Hot Tip

The rules governing property names are the same as those for all identifiers; *see* page 157.

5. Save your work. If you launch the page in your web browser then you won't see any visual output, but that's OK; for now this is as much a coding exercise as anything else. Rest assured that the objects have been created and are stored in memory ready for the page to use. We'll be doing much more with objects in Chapter 5.

Above: Firefox's Web Console tool (look in the browser's Tools menu) lets us confirm that the three objects have been loaded into memory.

ACCESSING OBJECT PROPERTIES

If we have an object (myObject) on which we've defined a property (myProperty) then we can access that property's value by typing myObject.myProperty. The full stop is called the **dot operator** (*see* page 174). The dot operator is used widely in JavaScript; you started using it way back on page 54 when coding a window.alert() command.

```
21
22        var highestEverScore = player1.maxScore;
23
```

Above: Accessing the value stored in an object property is very easy.

EXPRESSIONS AND OPERATORS

The instructions you write in scripts are made up of expressions. Typically, expressions use operators to manipulate data in some way.

WHAT IS AN EXPRESSION?

An expression is any segment of code that the interpreter can evaluate (evaluate means to process and create a value from it). This is actually a very simple concept. Take a look at this number literal:

42

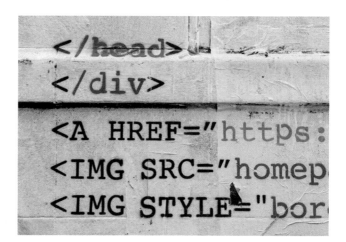

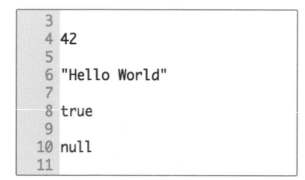

Above: The interpreter can evaluate all of these expressions... they're all utterly pointless though.

Strictly speaking, as well as being a literal this is also an expression: the interpreter can read it, and will return the value 42. Of course, this isn't much of an expression, it's the scripting equivalent of walking up to a friend and saying 'forty two'; she will understand what you've said, but she won't have a clue what you expect her to do with the information!

Becoming More Expressive

Now look at this expression: 38 + 4. This time, when evaluating the expression, the interpreter will add 38 and 4 – the result is the same as before, the value 42, but we have achieved something by adding the two values together. It's like you've said to your friend 'Thirty-eight plus four', to which she's replied 'Forty-two'. The thing that made the difference was the inclusion of the **addition operator**, +.

```
 2
 3  38 + 4
 4
 5  "Hello " + "World"
 6
 7  myVariable = true
 8
 9  quizQuestion.questionText
10
11  myObject.doSomething()
12
13  value1 < value2
14
15  true && false
16
```

WHAT IS AN OPERATOR?

As we've just seen, for an expression to have a purpose, it needs to include an operator; the operator defines what should be done with the data in the expression in order to obtain a value from the expression.

Left: Operators give meaning and purpose to expressions.

Hot Tip

A complete listing of JavaScript's operators can be found at https://en.wikibooks. org/wiki/JavaScript/Operators

Operands

When talking about operators, the value(s) being processed are referred to as **operands**. Many operators expect two operands, one written on either side of the operator, referred to as the left and right operands. Others operate on only one operand, whilst a very few work with three or more operands.

OODLES OF OPERATORS

There are many different JavaScript operators, too many to cover here, but let's take a look at the essential ones.

The Dot Operator

We've already met the dot operator. It allows us to access the properties (and methods, *see* page 194) of objects. The left operand is a reference to an object, the right the name of a property (or method) of that object.

ARITHMETIC OPERATORS

These operators perform an arithmetic calculation – addition, subtraction, multiplication or division – on the supplied operands and returns the result of that calculation. The operands must be numbers, or expressions that evaluate to numbers.

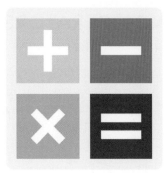

Operator	Name	Number of operands	Action	Example (result in brackets)
+	Addition	2	Sums the left and right operands	4 + 5 (9)
-	Subtraction	2	Subtracts the right operand from the left operand	31 - 14 (17)
*	Multiplication	2	Multiplies the left and right operands	12 * 3 (36)
/	Division	2	Divides the left operand by the right operand	12 / 3 (4)
++	Increment	1	Adds 1 to the operand	numUsers ++ (numUsers increases by 1)
- -	Decrement	1	Subtracts 1 from the operand	numUsers - - (numUsers decreases by 1)

STRING OPERATORS

There are a few different operators that can work with strings, but only one dedicated to strings:

Operator	Name	Number of operands	Action	Example (result in brackets)
+	Concatenate	2	Joins two strings together, returning the resulting string	`"Hello " + "World" ("Hello World")`

As you can see, the concatenate operator looks the same as the addition operator. The interpreter works out which operator is intended based on the data types of the operands. If both operands are numbers then + is addition; if either operand is a string then + is concatenate. Also, if an operand of the concatenate operator is a number then that number is automatically converted to a string, for example 74 would become "74".

ASSIGNMENT OPERATOR

We've already met this operator whose left operand is always a variable or property reference, and whose right operand can be any literal, identifier or expression.

Operator	Name	Number of operands	Action	Example (result in brackets)
=	Assignment	2	Assigns the value of the right operand to the variable or property indicated by the left operand	`myVar = 42` (myVar now has a value of 42)

EQUALITY OPERATORS

These operators compare two operands and return either `true` or `false` (*see* Booleans on page 163). The operands can be of any datatype.

Operator	Name	Number of operands	Action	Example (result in brackets)
==	Equality	2	Returns true if the two operands are equal, otherwise false	`4 == 2` (`false`)
!=	Inequality	2	Returns true if the two operands are not equal, otherwise false	`4 != 2` (`true`)

COMPARISON OPERATORS

Comparison operators, as the name suggests, compare two operands and return either `true` or `false`. The operands can be of any datatype.

Operator	Name	Number of operands	Action	Example (result in brackets)
 <=	less than / less than or equal	2	Returns true if the left operand's value is less than (or equal to) the right operand's value, otherwise false	`52 < 20 (false)` `19 <= 19 (true)`
> >=	greater than / greater than or equal	2	Returns true if the left operand's value is greater than (or equal to) the right operand's value, otherwise false	`52 > 20 (true)` `52 >= 100 (false)`

LOGICAL OPERATORS

Logical operators compare two Boolean values and then return either `true` or `false`. The operands are converted to Booleans if required.

Operator	Name	Number of operands	Action	Example (result in brackets)
&&	logical AND	2	Returns true if both operands evaluate to true, otherwise false	`true && false (false)`
||	logical OR	2	Returns true if either operand evaluates to true, otherwise false	`true || false (true)`
!	logical NOT	1	Placed before its single operand; inverts the Boolean value of the operand	`!true (false)` `!false (true)`

OPERATOR PRECEDENCE

Take a look at the following code:
4 * 12 - 9. Does this mean
(4 * 12) - 9, which would
evaluate to 39, or could it mean 4 *
(12 - 9), which would evaluate to
12? JavaScript deals with this by giving
every operator a number ranking, known
as the operator's **precedence**. The
operator with the highest precedence
is evaluated first; the operator with the
lowest precedence, last. Why not write
a script to see which of the above is the
correct solution.

```
11    <script type="text/javascript">
12
13        var actualResult = 4 * 12 - 9;
14        window.alert("4 * 12 - 9 equals " + actualResult);
15        var possResult1 = (4 * 20) - 9;
16        window.alert("(4 * 20) - 9 equals " + possResult1);
17        var possResult2 = 4 * (20 - 9);
18        window.alert("4 * (20 - 9) equals " + possResult2);
19
20    </script>
```

Above: Here we explore JavaScript's operator precedence rules. Try this script for yourself.

Overriding Operator Precedence

Remembering the precedence of every operator can be quite challenging. It's often
easier to override the default operator precedence using brackets – or **parentheses**,
as they're called in JavaScript.

Any expression contained within parentheses will be evaluated before all other expressions in the same statement (*see* opposite page). For example, take a look at this code: $(24 - 2) / 7$. Firstly, $(24 - 2)$ will be evaluated and the result, 22, will then be divided by 7.

Hot Tip

When nesting parentheses always be sure that each opening parenthesis, (, is matched by a closing parenthesis,) . A syntax error will occur if there's a mismatch.

Nesting Parentheses

There are many situations in which you will need to nest parentheses within parentheses, for example $((24 -2) + 10) / 7$. When you do this, it's the deepest nested expression that will be evaluated first, followed by the next deepest nested, and so on.

Below: The second variable declaration has a syntax error.

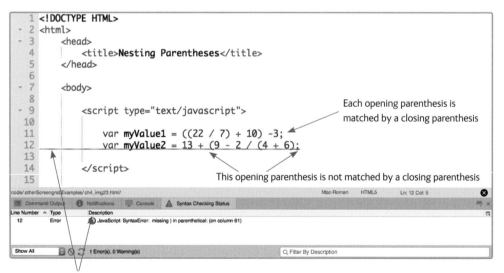

```
1  <!DOCTYPE HTML>
2  <html>
3      <head>
4          <title>Nesting Parentheses</title>
5      </head>
6
7      <body>
8
9          <script type="text/javascript">
10
11              var myValue1 = ((22 / 7) + 10) -3;
12              var myValue2 = 13 + (9 - 2 / (4 + 6);
13
14          </script>
15
```

Each opening parenthesis is matched by a closing parenthesis

This opening parenthesis is not matched by a closing parenthesis

code/ otherScreengrabExamples/ ch4_img23.html/   Mac-Roman   HTML5   Ln: 12 Col: 5

Line Number ∧	Type	Description
12	Error	JavaScript: SyntaxError: missing) in parenthetical: (on column 61)

Command Output · Notifications · Console · Syntax Checking Status

Show All   1 Error(s), 0 Warning(s)   Q Filter By Description

IDE has detected the syntax error caused by the missing parenthesis.

STATEMENTS

A JavaScript statement contains one or more expressions, and can be thought of as an individual step or instruction within a script. Each statement in a script is executed fully before the next statement is processed.

MAKING A STATEMENT

Take a look at the following simple expression:

```
playerScore = 0;
```

Whilst this is an expression, it is also a statement because it is a single instruction that ends with a semicolon.

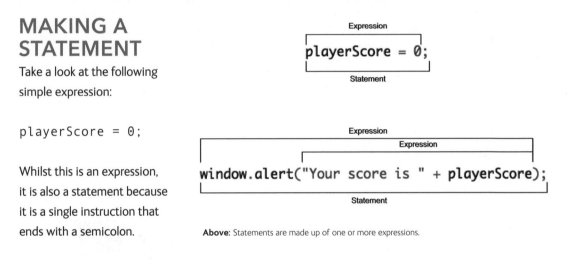

Above: Statements are made up of one or more expressions.

Combining Expressions

We often build up quite complicated stacks of expressions within a statement – just take a look at the statement in the image below. This rather scary looking lump of code actually achieves a very simple result. Running it after a page has loaded will create a paragraph containing the words 'Hello World'.

```
document.getElementsByTagName("body")[0].appendChild(document.createElement("p")).innerHTML = "Hello World!";
```

Above: Statements can end up looking quite daunting, but are often much easier to write than to read.

A Matter of Taste

It's important to understand that a lengthy and complicated statement, such as the one we've just looked at, can quite easily be broken down into a series of shorter, simpler statements. How you do things is, in most circumstances, a matter of personal preference.

```
25
26    var bodyElement = document.getElementsByTagName("body")[0];
27    var newParagraph = document.createElement("p");
28    newParagraph.innerHTML = "Hello World!";
29    bodyElement.appendChild(newParagraph);
30
```

Above: Whether to chain together lots of expressions or not is a matter of taste; these four statements do exactly the same thing as the previous scary looking single statement.

STATEMENT BLOCKS

Related statements can be grouped together into a block. This is done by wrapping the statements in curly brackets (known as braces in JavaScript). For example:

```
{
    var playerScore = 0;
    var playerName = 'Emma';
    var playerAge = 15;
}
```

This technique has its uses but doesn't really achieve an awful lot. But, as we are about to see, statement blocks become increasingly important the deeper we delve into JavaScript.

EXERCISE 13: if STATEMENTS

We often need to have our scripts make decisions based on conditions that don't exist until a page has been loaded into a browser and a user is interacting with it. This is when we reach for conditional statements, such as if.

WHAT IS AN if STATEMENT?

An if statement tests to see if a particular condition is true, and if so it executes a statement block. Its general form looks like this:

```
if ( condition ) {
    statement(s);
}
```

How if Statements Work

When the interpreter encounters an if statement it evaluates the expression contained inside the brackets. If that expression evaluates to true then the statement block following the if is executed.

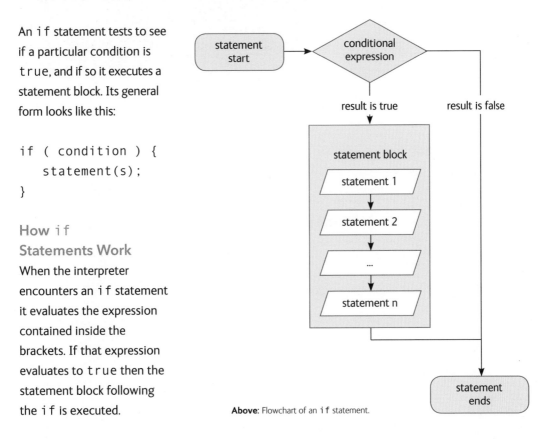

Above: Flowchart of an if statement.

USING if STATEMENTS

1. Let's see how an if statement works using a simple example. Create a new HTML document and add the standard structural elements, `<html>`, `<head>` and `<body>`. Also add a `<script type="text/javascript">` element inside `<body>`. Save the page as ifExample.htm

```
<html>
  <body>
    <img src="i_love_programming">
  </body>
</html>
```

```
 1  <!DOCTYPE HTML>
 2
 3  <html>
 4
 5      <head>
 6          <title>If Example</title>
 7      </head>
 8
 9      <body>
10
11          <script type="text/javascript">
12
13          </script>
14
15      </body>
16
17  </html>
```

Above: As a starting point, create an HTML page with a `<script>` element inside its `<body>`.

2. We met the `window` object all the way back on page 54, where we used its `alert()` method; you've also met the dot operator that allows us to access the properties and methods of objects (methods are covered on page 194). This time we're going to use the `prompt()` method of the `window` object; this creates a popup box into which the user can enter a value.

3. When the user enters a value in the prompt popup and clicks OK, that value becomes the value of the `window.prompt()` expression, and so we can assign it to a variable. It's a string variable, and so we also need to convert it to a number. Add the code shown in Figure 13-1 below.

```
12
13          var userAge = window.prompt("Please enter your age");
14          userAge = Number(userAge);
15
```

Above: Figure 13-1: Add this to your script element. The `Number` function converts the string value returned by `window.prompt()` into a number.

4. Now we need to test the value that was entered: we do this with an `if` statement. Add the following code to your script:

```
if (userAge > 18) {
}
```

5. We need to write some statements that will execute in the `if`'s statement block. We'll keep it simple: enter the code shown in Figure 13-2 below.

```
15
16          if (userAge > 18) {
17              window.alert("This is a kids-only zone - adults not allowed!");
18          }
19
```

Above: Figure 13-2: Add the `if` statement's statement block to your code.

6. Save your work and open ifExample.htm in your web browser. Reload the page a few times, entering different values in the prompt popup (be sure to enter a value over 18 if you want to see something happen).

How it Works

The page asks the user to enter a value for their age and this is stored in a variable called userAge. The if statement compares userAge against the literal value 18. If userAge is greater than 18 then the window.alert() statement is triggered.

Hot Tip

Try adding an else clause to the previous step-by-step exercise.

THE else CLAUSE

The next step up in the if statement is to add something called an else clause (it's called a clause because it's part of if and has no meaning outside of if). The general form looks like this:

```
if(condition) {
    statement(s);
} else {
    statement(s);
}
```

The statement block following else will execute when the if statement's condition evaluates to false.

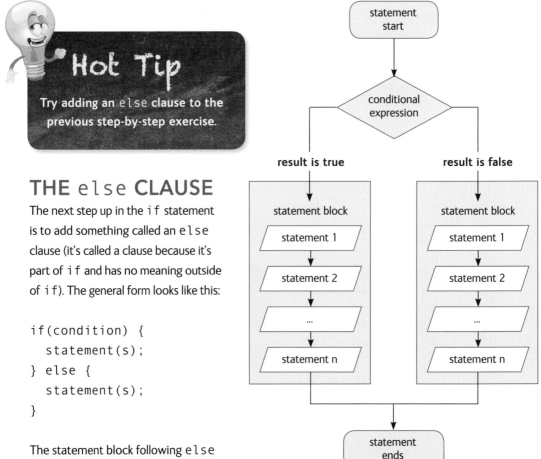

Above: Flow of an if statement with an else clause.

THE else if CLAUSE

A variant of the else clause is the else if clause. Just like else, else if is triggered when the if statement's conditional expression evaluates to false. However else if then introduces a new conditional test. The general form looks like this:

```
if (condition) {
    statement(s);
} else if (condition) {
    statement(s);
}
```

We can add as many else if clauses as we like, and also finish with a final else clause that executes if all other conditions have evaluated to false.

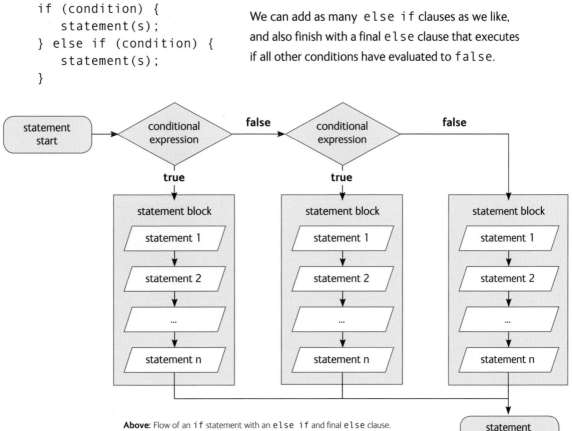

Above: Flow of an if statement with an else if and final else clause.

Nesting if Statements

if statements create a branching logical structure that's very common in programming. But beware: such structures become increasingly unwieldy with each additional branch.

EXERCISE 14: **FUNCTIONS**

Functions are collections of statements that are assigned to an identifier, and that can be triggered by using that identifier in a script. They allow us to create reusable blocks of code that can be called on when needed.

CALLING FUNCTIONS

When we write a function's name in a script and follow it with parentheses (brackets), we are **calling** or **invoking** the function. Using these parentheses we can also pass data, referred to as **arguments**, to the function.

Function Call Arguments

Arguments are values that are passed in a **function call**, and which the function can make use of. For example if calling the built-in `parseInt()` function, which converts a string into a number, we place the string to be converted within the parentheses. If passing more than one argument to a function, each is separated by a comma.

```
1
2  function showMessageToUser(userName, message) {
3      window.alert("Hi " + userName + ", " + message);
4  }
5
6  showMessageToUser("Emma", "Your function is working");
7
```

Above: A simple function definition and a call to that function.

NAMED FUNCTIONS

There are a couple of different techniques for creating functions, but the first is easy: we use the `function` keyword. It looks like this:

```
function functionName(parameter_1, parameter_2, ... , parameter_n)
{
  statement(s);
}
```

`functionName` is the name given to the function – it must follow the rules for identifier naming (*see* page 157). Then, within parentheses, we list the **parameters** of the function. Parameters are identifier names that receive the arguments contained in the function call; we can use these parameter names within the function to refer to the data passed to the function. A statement block follows the parentheses: this is known as the body of the function, and will be executed whenever the function is invoked.

Hot Tip

When passing data in a function call, the arguments must be listed in the same order as the parameter names are listed in the function definition.

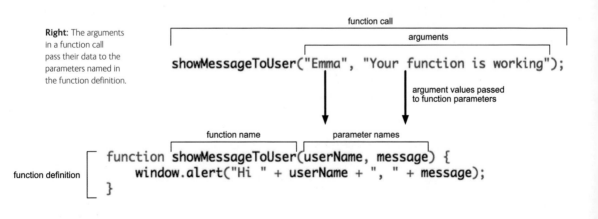

Right: The arguments in a function call pass their data to the parameters named in the function definition.

USING FUNCTIONS

1. In your code editor or IDE, create a new HTML file and save it as javascriptFunctions.htm. Add the basic required HTML elements to the document.

2. Create a new `<script>` element (don't forget the `type` attribute) in the `<head>` of the document (*see* Figure 14-1). We're going to define two functions here: one that gathers two numbers from the user, and the other that calculates a rectangular area from those numbers.

```
 1  <!DOCTYPE HTML>
 2
 3  <html>
 4      <head>
 5
 6          <script type="text/javascript">
 7
 8          </script>
 9
10      </head>
11
12      <body>
13
14      </body>
15
16  </html>
```

Above: Figure 14-1: Create a basic HTML document structure, and add a `<script>` element inside the `<head>`.

3. Within the `<script>` element, add the function definition code shown in Figure 14-2, below. This uses the `window.prompt()` method (*see* Methods on page 194) to gather two values from the user. It then uses the built-in `parseInt()` function to convert the strings returned by `window.prompt()` into numbers. Finally, the two numbers are placed into an array and then **returned** to the calling expression (we discuss `return` on page 192).

```
 7
 8  function askUserForValues() {
 9      var val1 = window.prompt("Please enter a width");
10      val1 = parseInt(val1);
11      var val2 = window.prompt("Please enter a height");
12      val2 = parseInt(val2);
13      var theResult = new Array(val1, val2);
14      return(theResult);
15  }
16
```

Above: Figure 14-2: Enter this function definition into the `<head>` element's `<script>` element.

4. Below the askUserForValues() function, add the calculateRectArea() function definition shown in Figure 14-3 below. This simple function has two parameters, width and height, which it multiplies together and returns to the calling expression.

```
16
17     function calculateRectArea(width, height) {
18         return(width * height);
19     }
20
```

Above: Figure 14-3: In the <body> script, add the function calls as shown here.

5. Add a new <script> element within the <body> of the HTML document.

6. Add the code shown in Figure 14-4 (below) to the new <script> element. The first statement calls the askUserForValues() function and stores the returned value in an array variable called dimensions. The second statement calls the calculateRectArea() function, passing the dimension values as arguments (notice how the arguments extract each value from the dimensions array). Finally, the third statement reports the results to the user via a window. alert() call (notice the use of the concatenate operator, +, discussed on page 176).

7. Save your work and open javascriptFunctions.htm in your browser.

```
26    <body>
27
28        <script type="text/javascript">
29
30            var dimensions = askUserForValues();
31            var rectArea = calculateRectArea(dimensions[0], dimensions[1]);
32            window.alert("A rectangle with a width of " + dimensions[0] +
33                         " and a height of " + dimensions[1] +
34                         " has an area of " + rectArea);
35
36        </script>
37
38    </body>
```

Above: Figure 14-4: Add in the funtion calls here to the <body> script.

The `return` Keyword

We've just met the `return` keyword for the first time. When the interpreter encounters `return` it ceases processing of the function and returns to the calling expression. If the function needs to send a value back to the calling expression then we place the value in parentheses following `return`, for example `return(functionResult);`.

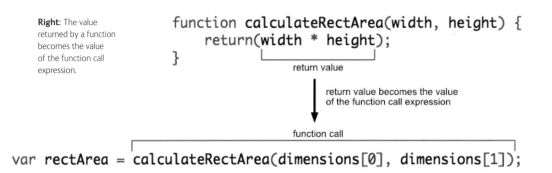

Right: The value returned by a function becomes the value of the function call expression.

```
function calculateRectArea(width, height) {
    return(width * height);
}
```

return value

return value becomes the value of the function call expression

function call

```
var rectArea = calculateRectArea(dimensions[0], dimensions[1]);
```

ANONYMOUS FUNCTIONS

In JavaScript a function is just another form of data. This means that you can create a function and assign it to a variable or object property. Such functions are called **anonymous functions** because they don't have a function name.

Declaring an Anonymous Function

We declare an anonymous function by assigning a **function literal** to a variable or object property. The general form looks like this:

```
var myAnonymousFunction = function(parameters) {
    statement(s);
}
```

Invoking an Anonymous Function

Invoking an anonymous function is no different to invoking a named one; we just use a variable name or property reference instead of a function name. To all intents and purposes this is identical to invoking a named function.

```
1  //This is a named function...
2  function calculateRectArea(rectWidth, rectHeight) {
3      return(rectWidth * rectHeight);
4  }
5
6  //This is an anonymous function...
7  var calculateRectHypotenuse = function(rectWidth, rectHeight) {
8      var widthSquared = rectWidth * rectWidth;
9      var heightSquared = rectHeight * rectHeight;
10     return(Math.sqrt(widthSquared + heightSquared)); //Math.sqrt() calculates a square root
11 }
12
13 //Calls to either function have the same general form:
14 var myRectArea = calculateRectArea(49, 28);
15 var myRectHypotenuse = calculateRectHypotenuse(49, 28);
16
```

Above: Named and anonymous functions are called in the same way.

CLASSES

In programming there is a concept called a **class**. A class is a collection of values and scripts that is used to represent something. For example, somebody coding a driving game may develop a car class to represent all of the cars in the game; each time the game needs a new car on the screen it will create, or **instantiate**, an object based on the car class. The object created isn't the car class, it's an instance of the car class: a car object, in other words.

As well as allowing you to write your own classes, JavaScript has a number of built-in classes, some of which we've already used (String, Number, Array and so on are all classes built-in to JavaScript, for example). So whilst we aren't going to be delving into the world of classes it's still important to be aware of them.

METHODS

A method is very similar to a function, except that it is defined as part of a class. Where a function is intended as a standalone object that works on data passed to it, a method is part and parcel of an object and, normally, performs actions that access and/or change that object in some way.

Hot Tip

Classes and methods are part of an approach to writing and structuring code called Object Oriented Programming, or *OOP*. The OOP approach is very widely used by developers.

```
 1  var com;
 2  if (!com) {
 3      com = new Object();
 4  }
 5  if (!com.flametreepublishing) {
 6      com.flametreepublishing = new Object();
 7  }
 8  if (!com.flametreepublishing.cfk) {
 9      com.flametreepublishing.cfk = new Object();
10  }
11
12  com.flametreepublishing.cfk.StarfleetDefence = function() {
13      this.maxFleetSize = 5;
14      this.fleet = new Array();
15      this.shotList = new Array();
16      this.craftDestroyed = 0;
17      this.currentMessage = "Enemy spacecraft detected in your quadrant! Find and destroy them using as few shots as
        possible.</br>Good luck commander!";
18      this.currentScore = 0;
19      this.bestScore = this.getBestScore();
20      this.gameOver = false;
21      this.audioPlayer = document.createElement("audio");
22  }
23
24  com.flametreepublishing.cfk.StarfleetDefence.prototype.getBestScore = function() {
25      var bestScoreFromCookie;
26      var allCookies = document.cookie;
27      var pos = allCookies.indexOf("bestScore=");
28      if (pos == -1) {
29          document.cookie = "bestScore=100; max-age=" + (60*60*24*365);
30          bestScoreFromCookie = 100;
31      } else {
```

Above: JavaScript allows you to create your own custom classes.

DYNAMIC HTML AND THE DOM

All modern web browsers support Dynamic HTML (DHTML), which allows JavaScript to make changes to a page after it has been loaded and rendered in the browser, with those changes shown immediately onscreen.

```
45
46  com.flametreepublishing.cfk.CodeSymbol.prototype.getHtmlElement = function() {
47      var wrapperElement = document.createElement("div");
48      wrapperElement.className = "codeSymbol";
49      var borderElement = document.createElement("div");
50      borderElement.className = "buttonBorder " + this.color;
51      var symbolWrapper = document.createElement("div");
52      symbolWrapper.className = "symbolGraphicWrapper";
53      symbolWrapper.style.position = "relative";
54      symbolWrapper.style.left = String(this.offset.x) + "px";
55      symbolWrapper.style.top = String(this.offset.y) + "px";
56      symbolWrapper.style.width = String(this.size.w) + "px";
57      symbolWrapper.style.height = String(this.size.h) + "px";
58      symbolWrapper.innerHTML = this.svg;
59      borderElement.appendChild(symbolWrapper);
60      wrapperElement.appendChild(borderElement);
61      return(wrapperElement);
62  }
63
```

Above: DHTML and DOM programming allow us to make extensive changes to a page after it's loaded into a browser.

WHAT IS THE DOM?

We know that HTML creates a nested, or hierarchical, structure of elements. JavaScript allows us to create similar hierarchical structures by storing objects within objects and, as it turns out, this is exactly what a web browser generates from the source HTML code. This internal representation, or model, of the page is known as the **Document Object Model**, or **DOM** for short, and we can use JavaScript to dig into that model and change, well, pretty much anything we like!

DOM PROGRAMMING

JavaScript's DOM classes, such as HTMLDocument and HTMLElement, provide numerous methods for manipulating a loaded page, and give access to properties that directly map to HTML attributes. For example, a <p> element is represented in the DOM by an HTMLElement object; any attributes defined on the <p> element are available to JavaScript as properties of the HTMLElement object, and vice versa.

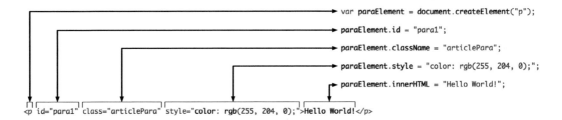

Above: Attributes of an HTML element become properties of the corresponding DOM object, and vice versa.

EVENTS

Events are messages issued by the browser in response to a user interaction or some other condition. An event always has a type which indicates the nature of the event. For example, clicking on any element in a page causes that element to send, or **dispatch**, an event of type "click".

Event Listeners and Handlers

If we want our scripts to respond to an event, we have to write code that listens for that event occurring: this code is called an **event listener**. Typically, when triggered, an event listener calls another function referred to as the event handler, which performs actions in response to the event.

ONWARDS

We've flown over a huge amount of ground in this chapter, and not all of it has been simple or straightforward, but this is to be expected. JavaScript is a deep subject! Don't worry though, because the next, and final, chapter features loads of hands-on practical examples of all of the JavaScript we've covered so far, as well as how it all fits together with everything you've learned about HTML and CSS too.

PLAYING WITH CODE

EXERCISE 15:
STARFLEET DEFENCE

Enemy spacecraft have been detected in your quadrant! Find and destroy
them using as few shots as possible. Good luck, commander!

GAME OVERVIEW

Starfleet Defence is a single-player game in which the aim is to destroy the hidden enemy fleet
in as few shots as possible. There are five spacecraft of varying sizes to find and destroy.

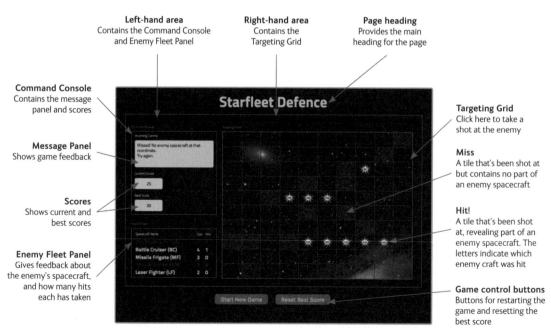

Left-hand area
Contains the Command Console
and Enemy Fleet Panel

Right-hand area
Contains the
Targeting Grid

Page heading
Provides the main
heading for the page

Command Console
Contains the message
panel and scores

Message Panel
Shows game feedback

Scores
Shows current and
best scores

Enemy Fleet Panel
Gives feedback about
the enemy's spacecraft,
and how many hits
each has taken

Targeting Grid
Click here to take a
shot at the enemy

Miss
A tile that's been shot at
but contains no part of
an enemy spacecraft

Hit!
A tile that's been shot
at, revealing part of an
enemy spacecraft. The
letters indicate which
enemy craft was hit

Game control buttons
Buttons for restarting the
game and resetting the
best score

Above: Take a look at the Starfleet Defence game screen and familiarize yourself with the various panels it creates and uses.

Coding the Game

For Starfleet Defence we will focus mainly on the process of building the HTML structure and responding to events in the game, and so we've provided the CSS and a lot of the JavaScript code that the game needs. Once you've finished the other game projects you should come back and study this code, which includes notes and comments to help you to understand it.

Hot Tip

When creating a wireframe, one approach is to label the different areas of the wireframe using a CSS-like notation. Color-coding different levels of nesting also helps to highlight the HTML structure.

WIREFRAMING

When planning a web page, one of the first stages is to create a **wireframe** drawing of the page. This is a great way of working out the HTML structure of the page, and for planning the CSS selectors and style rules you'll need. Your graphics editor is a good tool for wireframing, but you can use whatever you like: a pencil and paper will do!

From Wireframe to HTML

Take a look at the wireframe on the right (also provided as a PDF file in the Exercise 15 folder of the downloadable code package). The wireframe illustrates how the HTML elements need to be nested and structured, and allows us to plan the CSS selectors that will be required too.

Above: A wireframe design can be a big help in planning and understanding a page's layout.

PREPARING THE PROJECT FOLDER

The starting point for this game is contained in the downloadable code package as Exercise15\startingPoint\StarfleetDefence\. Copy this folder to your working folder or other convenient hard drive location.

Above: Your StarfleetDefence project folder should look like this.

CREATING THE BASIC STRUCTURE

1. Open StarfleetDefence.htm in your code editor; we've already added the basic required HTML elements for you.

2. In the `<head>`, add a `<title>` element, as in figure 15-1. Remember, this is the title that will appear on the browser window's frame or tab.

```
 1  <!DOCTYPE HTML>
 2
 3  <html>
 4
 5      <head>
 6          <meta charset="utf-8"/>
 7          <title>Starfleet Defence</title>
 8      </head>
 9
10      <body>
11
12      </body>
13
```

Above: Figure 15-1: Add the `<title>` element to the basic page structure.

```
8
9       <link rel="stylesheet" type="text/css" href="css/StarfleetDefence.css"/>
10      <script type="text/javascript" src="js/TargetingCoordinate.js"></script>
11      <script type="text/javascript" src="js/Spacecraft.js"></script>
12      <script type="text/javascript" src="js/StarfleetDefence.js"></script>
13      <script type="text/javascript" src="js/gameControl.js"></script>
14
```

Above: Figure 15-2: Link to the external CSS and JavaScript files.

3. We need to link the page to the supporting JavaScript and CSS files. To do this, add the code shown in figure 15-2 to the <head> element.

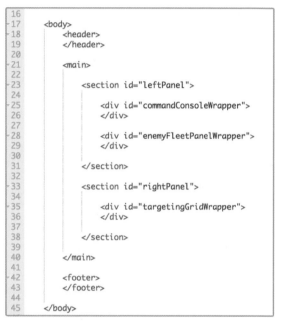

```
16
17      <body>
18          <header>
19          </header>
20
21          <main>
22
23              <section id="leftPanel">
24
25                  <div id="commandConsoleWrapper">
26                  </div>
27
28                  <div id="enemyFleetPanelWrapper">
29                  </div>
30
31              </section>
32
33              <section id="rightPanel">
34
35                  <div id="targetingGridWrapper">
36                  </div>
37
38              </section>
39
40          </main>
41
42          <footer>
43          </footer>
44
45      </body>
```

4. Our wireframe shows us the structure of the page, so let's translate that into HTML. Move to the <body> element of your page and then add the structural elements shown in figure 15-3.

Above: Figure 15-3: Start building the basic structure of the page; take a look at the wireframe to see how the HTML relates to it.

5. We need the game's title to appear at the top of the page; this will be the main heading on the page, so we'll use an <h1> for it. Add the following within the <header> element:

```
<h1>Starfleet
Defence</h1>.
```

Hot Tip

We often use <div> elements to create wrappers for sets of related elements. Doing this can be a big help when setting up the layout in CSS.

6. The Command Console area of the screen will show messages to the player, as well as the player's current score and the best score. Take a look at the wireframe to see how this is structured, and then create the elements, as shown in figure 15-4.

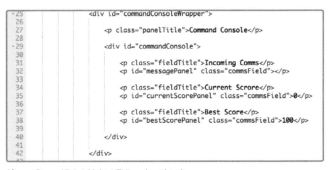

```
25      <div id="commandConsoleWrapper">
26
27          <p class="panelTitle">Command Console</p>
28
29          <div id="commandConsole">
30
31              <p class="fieldTitle">Incoming Comms</p>
32              <p id="messagePanel" class="commsField"></p>
33
34              <p class="fieldTitle">Current Scrore</p>
35              <p id="currentScorePanel" class="commsField">0</p>
36
37              <p class="fieldTitle">Best Score</p>
38              <p id="bestScorePanel" class="commsField">100</p>
39
40          </div>
41
42      </div>
```

Above: Figure 15-4: Add this HTML code within the `<div id="commandConsoleWrapper">` element.

7. The Enemy Fleet area of the screen will show a readout of the enemy spacecraft, how large they are, and how many hits they've received. To start with, add the elements as shown in Figure 15-5 within the

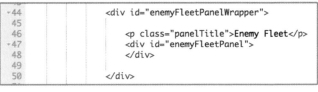

```
44              <div id="enemyFleetPanelWrapper">
45
46                  <p class="panelTitle">Enemy Fleet</p>
47                  <div id="enemyFleetPanel">
48                  </div>
49
50              </div>
```

Above: Figure 15-5: Add the elements shown within the `<div id="enemyFleetPanelWrapper">` element.

`<div id="enemyFleetPanelWrapper">` element.

8. We're going to use a table to display the list of enemy spacecraft (*see* page 77 for more on tables). Add the `<table>` element shown in Figure 15-6 within the `<div id="enemyFleetPanel">` element.

Right: Figure 15-6: Create this basic `<table>` element (and its child elements) which will display enemy fleet information.

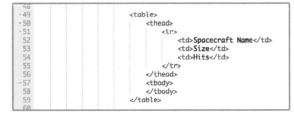

```
48
49                  <table>
50                      <thead>
51                          <tr>
52                              <td>Spacecraft Name</td>
53                              <td>Size</td>
54                              <td>Hits</td>
55                          </tr>
56                      </thead>
57                      <tbody>
58                      </tbody>
59                  </table>
60
```

9. We need to be able to target style rules at the table, and the easiest way of doing this is by giving it an ID, so give the `<table>` element an `id` attribute of `"enemyFleetPanelTable"`.

```
48
49    <table id="enemyFleetPanelTable">
50        <thead>
51            <tr>
52                <td>Spacecraft Name</td>
53                <td>Size</td>
54                <td>Hits</td>
55            </tr>
56        </thead>
57        <tbody id="enemyFleetPanelTableBody">
58        </tbody>
59    </table>
60
```

Above: Figure 15-7: Set unique `id` attribute values on the `<table>` and `<tbody>` elements.

10. The `<tbody>` element is currently empty. This is because JavaScript will add the elements here when the game starts, and update them as the game progresses.

    To make it easy to get hold of the `<tbody>` element from a script, give it an `id` of `"enemyFleetPanelTableBody"`.

11. That's everything prepared for the left-hand `<section>` element; your code should look similar to Figure 15-8.

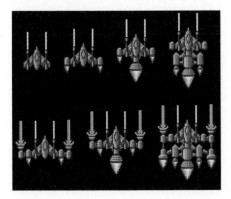

```
22
23    <section id="leftPanel">
24
25        <div id="commandConsoleWrapper">
26
27            <p class="panelTitle">Command Console</p>
28
29            <div id="commandConsole">
30
31                <p class="fieldTitle">Incoming Comms</p>
32                <p id="messagePanel" class="commsField"></p>
33
34                <p class="fieldTitle">Current Scrore</p>
35                <p id="currentScorePanel" class="commsField">0</p>
36
37                <p class="fieldTitle">Best Score</p>
38                <p id="bestScorePanel" class="commsField">100</p>
39
40            </div>
41
42        </div>
43
44        <div id="enemyFleetPanelWrapper">
45
46            <p class="panelTitle">Enemy Fleet</p>
47            <div id="enemyFleetPanel">
48
49                <table id="enemyFleetPanelTable">
50                    <thead>
51                        <tr>
52                            <td>Spacecraft Name</td>
53                            <td>Size</td>
54                            <td>Hits</td>
55                        </tr>
56                    </thead>
57                    <tbody id="enemyFleetPanelTableBody">
58                    </tbody>
59                </table>
60
61            </div>
62
63        </div>
64
65    </section>
66
```

Above: Figure 15-8: The complete HTML code for the left-hand panel.

12. Scroll down through your HTML document and find the right panel `<section>` element. We need to add the small title

```
▾67          <section id="rightPanel">
 68
▾69              <div id="targetingGridWrapper">
 70
 71                  <p class="panelTitle">Targeting Panel</p>
 72
 73              </div>
 74
 75          </section>
```

Above: Figure 15-9: Add the `<p>` element that will act as a small title above the targeting grid.

that sits above the actual targeting grid: add the `<p>` element shown in Figure 15-9 within the `<div id="targetingGridWrapper">` element.

13. The Targeting Grid itself will be a `<table>` with 10 rows, and 10 cells per row. That's 100 `<td>` elements in total, which would be very tedious to type out manually, so JavaScript will generate the table for us instead (see the `buildTargetingGrid()` method in the StarfleetDefence class file, StarfleetDefence.js).

Right: The Targeting Grid is actually a `<table>` element containing 100 `<td>` table cell elements: you don't want to be coding all of that by hand!

14. We've provided some sound effects to go with the different outcomes of the player taking a shot. JavaScript does not contain any mechanism for playing an audio file directly, but what it can do is control the playback of HTML `<audio>` elements.

Hot Tip

Preloading audio or video won't necessarily load the entire media file into the browser, but will tell it to load enough of the file to be able to begin playback on request.

15. After the right-hand `<section>`, create an `<audio>` element for each of the four sound effects. We don't want any visual output from these, nor do we want the sounds to play automatically, so don't include the `controls` or `autoplay` attributes. We do want the web browser to load these sounds so they're ready to play, so include a `preload="true"` attribute on each element. See Figure 15-10.

```
76
77        <audio preload="true"></audio>
78        <audio preload="true"></audio>
79        <audio preload="true"></audio>
80        <audio preload="true"></audio>
81
```

Above right: Figure 15-10: Add four `<audio>` elements below the second `<section>` element.

16. We've supplied each
sound effect as both
WAV and MP3 files.
Add the `<source>`
elements for these
to each `<audio>`
element, as shown
in Figure 15-11.

```
76
77      <audio preload="true">
78          <source src="sound/cantShoot.wav" type="audio/wav"/>
79          <source src="sound/cantShoot.mp3" type="audio/mpeg"/>
80      </audio>
81
82      <audio preload="true">
83          <source src="sound/shootAndMiss.wav" type="audio/wav"/>
84          <source src="sound/shootAndMiss.mp3" type="audio/mpeg"/>
85      </audio>
86
87      <audio preload="true">
88          <source src="sound/shootAndHit.wav" type="audio/wav"/>
89          <source src="sound/shootAndHit.mp3" type="audio/mpeg"/>
90      </audio>
91
92      <audio preload="true">
93          <source src="sound/shootAndDestroy.wav" type="audio/wav"/>
94          <source src="sound/shootAndDestroy.mp3" type="audio/mpeg"/>
95      </audio>
96
97  </main>
98
```

Above: Figure 15-11: Create `<source>` elements for each audio file.

17. Giving each
`<audio>` element
an ID will make it
much easier to get
hold of them from
JavaScript; we'll
give ours IDs that
start with "`sfx_`"
followed by the
name of the sound
file (without the file
extension). Figure
15-12 shows you what you should end up with.

```
77      <audio id="sfx_cantShoot" preload="true">
78          <source src="sound/cantShoot.wav" type="audio/wav"/>
79          <source src="sound/cantShoot.mp3" type="audio/mpeg"/>
80      </audio>
81
82      <audio id="sfx_shootAndMiss" preload="true">
83          <source src="sound/shootAndMiss.wav" type="audio/wav"/>
84          <source src="sound/shootAndMiss.mp3" type="audio/mpeg"/>
85      </audio>
86
87      <audio id="sfx_shootAndHit" preload="true">
88          <source src="sound/shootAndHit.wav" type="audio/wav"/>
89          <source src="sound/shootAndHit.mp3" type="audio/mpeg"/>
90      </audio>
91
92      <audio id="sfx_shootAndDestroy" preload="true">
93          <source src="sound/shootAndDestroy.wav" type="audio/wav"/>
94          <source src="sound/shootAndDestroy.mp3" type="audio/mpeg"/>
95      </audio>
```

Above: Figure 15-12: Give each `<audio>` element an ID so that it's easy to access with JavaScript.

18. Finally, we'll add the two buttons that appear at the bottom of the game screen. We'll use
`<button>` elements for this, and place these in the page's `<footer>`. The code for this
is shown in Figure 15-13.

Right: Figure 15-13: Add the `<button>` elements in the page's `<footer>` element.

```
98
99  <footer>
100
101     <button id="newGameButton" type="button">Start New Game</button>
102     <button id="resetBestScoreButton" type="button">Reset Best Score</button>
103
104 </footer>
105
```

19. Save your work. If you open the page in your browser you will see the basic layout starting to take shape. You should also study the StarfleetDefence.css file to see how the various elements you've created are being styled – the majority of the style properties used should be familiar to you (we'll look more closely at setting up a style sheet when we work on the next game).

Hot Tips

It may seem odd to have to set a `<button>` element's `type` attribute to "`button`"; this is to distinguish it from a button in a web form, whose type would be "`submit`" or "`reset`".

A LOT OF IDS

You will notice that we've set a lot of id attributes. These let us target style rules at the elements, of course, but they also serve to help with scripting. The `getElementByID()` method of the page's `document` object allows us to get hold of the element so that we can do things with it – such as, add or remove content, change styling and so on.

Right: The basic structure of the page is in place, but there's no game yet!

GAME CLASSES

We've linked the page to a number of scripts. The majority of these are class definition scripts (*see* page 193): when the page loads and the interpreter reads those class definitions, it creates a number of new object types that become available to the page, although it doesn't create any actual objects from the classes. You may like to take a look at the class scripts – go right ahead, but note that they use some techniques that we haven't covered.

The StarfleetDefence Class

This class represents the game itself – it's the game engine if you like. We need to generate one object, or instance, of this class, and store it in a variable that the whole page can access.

The Spacecraft Class

The Spacecraft class, as the name suggests, represents the enemy spacecraft in the game.

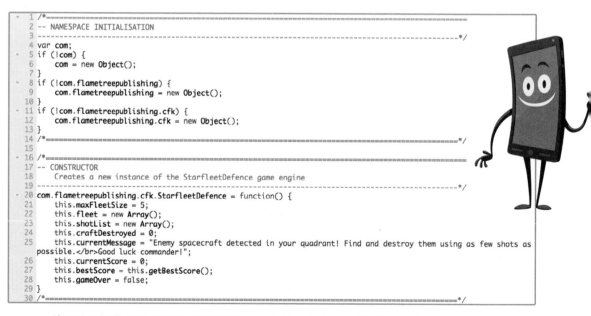

```
 1  /*=================================================================
 2  -- NAMESPACE INITIALISATION
 3  ---------------------------------------------------------------*/
 4  var com;
 5  if (!com) {
 6      com = new Object();
 7  }
 8  if (!com.flametreepublishing) {
 9      com.flametreepublishing = new Object();
10  }
11  if (!com.flametreepublishing.cfk) {
12      com.flametreepublishing.cfk = new Object();
13  }
14  /*=================================================================*/
15
16  /*=================================================================
17  -- CONSTRUCTOR
18      Creates a new instance of the StarfleetDefence game engine
19  ---------------------------------------------------------------*/
20  com.flametreepublishing.cfk.StarfleetDefence = function() {
21      this.maxFleetSize = 5;
22      this.fleet = new Array();
23      this.shotList = new Array();
24      this.craftDestroyed = 0;
25      this.currentMessage = "Enemy spacecraft detected in your quadrant! Find and destroy them using as few shots as
    possible.</br>Good luck commander!";
26      this.currentScore = 0;
27      this.bestScore = this.getBestScore();
28      this.gameOver = false;
29  }
30  /*=================================================================*/
```

Above: You should take a look at the class scripts, but don't expect to understand everything they contain.

Instances of the class store information about the craft's name, size, grid position and so on.

The TargetingCoordinate Class

The third class in the game represents a coordinate on the Targeting Grid. When you click on the grid a TargetingCoordinate object is created and then tested against the Spacecraft instances to see if the shot is a hit.

CONTROLLING THE GAME

1. We need to write scripts in order to work with the game's classes. We're going to write these scripts in the gameControl.js file, located in the js folder. Open this file in your code editor.

2. On the first line add the following variable declaration:

```
var gameEngine;
```

```
1 var gameEngine;
```

Above: Figure 15-14: Declare the gameEngine variable, which will be available to all of the page's scripts.

The variable is going to store an instance of the StarfleetDefence class and, because it's declared outside of a function or class definition, the variable, and therefore the class instance, will be available to any scripts running in the page.

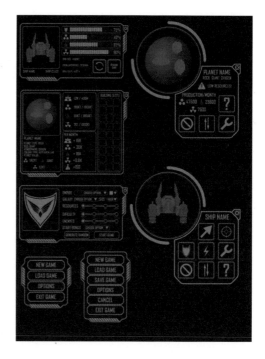

3. We haven't yet assigned a value to gameEngine because we need to be sure the whole page has loaded before doing so. When the page has completed loading it will issue an onload event (*see* page 196): we need to listen for that event.

4. The onload event is dispatched by the window object, and has an event type of "load". The event listener code for this is shown in Figure 15-15; add it to your script.

```
2
3 window.addEventListener("load", initialiseGame, false);
4
```

Above: Figure 15-15: This code will listen for the window object dispatching an onload event.

5. The first argument of the `addEventListener()` call specifies the event type to listen for whilst the second argument is the name of the function to call in response to the event (notice that we didn't include the parentheses after the function name). The third argument is a bit complicated. It tends to always be set to `false`, and that's all you need to know about it for now!

6. The listener calls a function called `initialiseGame()`. The code for this is shown in Figure 15-16; add it to your script. The first statement in the function creates a new instance of the StarfleetDefence class and assigns it to our `gameEngine` variable. The second statement calls a function called `startNewGame()`. Let's write that function now.

```
4
5 function initialiseGame() {
6     gameEngine = new com.flametreepublishing.cfk.StarfleetDefence();
7     startNewGame();
8 }
9
```

Above: Figure 15-16: This function will be called when the onload event listener is triggered.

7. Copy the function shown in Figure 15-17 to your script. The annotations explain what each statement does. Save the script when done.

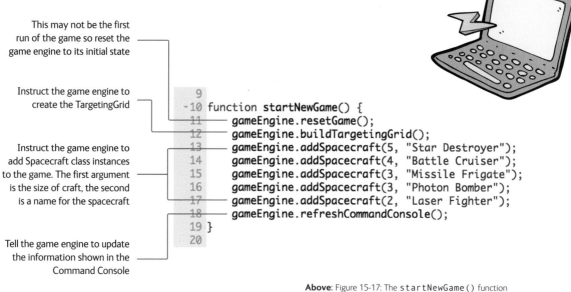

This may not be the first run of the game so reset the game engine to its initial state

Instruct the game engine to create the TargetingGrid

Instruct the game engine to add Spacecraft class instances to the game. The first argument is the size of craft, the second is a name for the spacecraft

Tell the game engine to update the information shown in the Command Console

```
 9
▾10 function startNewGame() {
 11     gameEngine.resetGame();
 12     gameEngine.buildTargetingGrid();
 13     gameEngine.addSpacecraft(5, "Star Destroyer");
 14     gameEngine.addSpacecraft(4, "Battle Cruiser");
 15     gameEngine.addSpacecraft(3, "Missile Frigate");
 16     gameEngine.addSpacecraft(3, "Photon Bomber");
 17     gameEngine.addSpacecraft(2, "Laser Fighter");
 18     gameEngine.refreshCommandConsole();
 19 }
 20
```

Above: Figure 15-17: The startNewGame() function resets any current game and then prepares a new one.

8. Switch over to the StarfleetDefence.htm document and locate the two <button> elements in the <footer>. We could write event listeners and handlers to deal with clicks on these buttons, but there is another, often simpler, way of handling things. On the first <button> add the following attribute and value:

onclick="startNewGame();"

What we've done here is tell the button to call the startNewGame() function in response to a click.

9. On the second button, add this attribute and value:

```
onclick="gameEngine.resetBestScore();"
```

This game engine method, when called, will reset the best score value to 100.

```
100
101    <button id="newGameButton" type="button" onclick="startNewGame();">Start New Game</button>
102
103    <button id="resetBestScoreButton" type="button" onclick="gameEngine.resetBestScore();">Reset Best Score</button>
104
```

Above: Figure 15-18: Set the onclick attribute of the two buttons.

10. Save the HTML page and flip back to the gameControl.js script.

TAKING THE SHOT

When the game engine created the Targeting Grid, it assigned a "click" event listener to each cell of the grid. Those listeners call an event handler function called takeShot(), which needs to evaluate whether the shot will hit a target and then perform appropriate actions depending on the result. Let's write the function.

Hot Tip

Long scripts can become difficult to navigate and finding specific functions or methods can get frustrating. One remedy is to use comments to create visual blocks and sections; you will see this technique in the supplied scripts for this exercise.

1. Write the shell of the function, as shown in Figure 15-19. The function will receive an object which contains information about the event that was triggered; we capture that argument as the eventObj parameter of the function.

```
20
21 function takeShot(eventObj) {
22
23 }
24
```

Above: Figure 15-19: Declare the takeShot() function.

2. If a game has completed, then we don't want anything to happen if the grid is clicked: the code in Figure 15-20 will take care of this for us, so add it to your script. It checks the gameOver property of the game engine, and drops out of the script if the property is true.

```
22    if (gameEngine.gameOver) {
23        return;
24    }
25
```

Above: Figure 15-20: We don't want the function to do anything if the game has actually finished. This code takes care of that.

3. The next thing we need to do is work out the coordinates that were clicked. The eventObj.target property is a reference to the clicked <td> element, which was given custom coordinate_x and coordinate_y attributes when it was created. The code in Figure 15-21 extracts the values of those attributes and then creates a new TargetingCoordinate instance to represent the clicked coordinate; add the code to your takeShot() function.

```
25    var clickedTDElement = eventObj.target;
26    var clickedX = clickedTDElement.getAttribute("coordinate_x");
27    var clickedY = clickedTDElement.getAttribute("coordinate_y");
28    var target = new com.flametreepublishing.cfk.TargetingCoordinate(clickedX, clickedY);
```

Above: Figure 15-21: This code works out the grid coordinates of the clicked <td>, and creates a new TargetingCoordinate object from them.

4. Passing the TargetingCoordinate to the game engine's `hitTest()` method instructs the engine to calculate the result of shooting at that coordinate; this is returned as a string. There are a few possible values that will be returned: `"oob"` (standing for 'out of bounds') if the coordinate is somehow garbled or doesn't make sense; `"repeat shot"` if the coordinate has already been shot at; `"miss"` if there is no spacecraft at the coordinate. Otherwise the method returns the name of the spacecraft that was hit. What we need is an `if` statement to handle the possible return values.

Hot Tip

The HTML `<br>` tag creates a line break within a paragraph (or other run) of text.

5. Figure 15-22 shows the call to `hitTest()` and the beginning of the if statement, which tests for the `"oob"` `hitTest()` result value. Copy the code to your script. The game engine's `playSound()` and `setMessage()` methods should be self-explanatory.

```
29    var hitTestResult = gameEngine.hitTest(target);
30    if (hitTestResult == "oob") {
31        gameEngine.playSound("sfx_cantShoot");
32        gameEngine.setMessage("The location you targeted is outside of your quadrant.<br>Try again.");
33    }
34
```

Above: Figure 15-22: Call the `hitTest()` method and then create an `if` statement to handle the result.

6. Next we'll add an `else if` clause to test for the "`repeat shot`" result:
   the code is shown in Figure 15-23.

```
33    } else if (hitTestResult == "repeat shot") {
34        gameEngine.playSound("sfx_cantShoot");
35        gameEngine.setMessage("You have already shot at that coordinate.<br>Try again.");
36    }
37
```

Above: Figure 15-23: This `else if` clause tests for the "`repeat shot`" result.

7. If the result of `hitTest()` is "`miss`" then we need to do a few things: we need
   to call `logShot()` to tell the game engine to store the TargetingCoordinate so that
   it can tell if the same coordinate gets clicked again; we need to add 1 to the current
   score by calling `updateCurrentScore()`; we need to play a sound effect and
   report a message like we have done previously; and finally, we need to make the
   clicked cell indicate visually that it was a miss, which we do by assigning CSS classes
   to it. The code to do all of these things is shown in Figure 15-24: add it to your script.

```
36    } else if (hitTestResult == "miss") {
37        gameEngine.logShot(target);
38        gameEngine.updateCurrentScore();
39        gameEngine.playSound("sfx_shootAndMiss");
40        gameEngine.setMessage("Missed! No enemy spacecraft at that coordinate.<br>Try again.");
41        clickedTDElement.className = "targetingGridCell missed";
42    }
43
```

Above: Figure 15-24: This `else if` clause deals with a `hitTest()` result of "`miss`".

8. If all of the `if-else-if` conditions we've tested so far have been `false` then we
   can assume `hitTest()` has returned the name of a spacecraft that intersects the
   coordinate. Adding a final `else` clause to our `if` statement will let us handle this
   hit condition.

9. We need to get the Spacecraft object that will be hit: the game engine will give us this if we call the `getSpacecraftByName()` method, passing as an argument the name of the spacecraft returned by `hitTest()`. Figure 15-25 shows the code.

```
42    } else {
43        var theSpacecraft = gameEngine.getSpacecraftByName(hitTestResult);
44
```

Above: Figure 15-25: Create a final else clause, and then get the Spacecraft object from the game engine.

10. Next, as in step 7, we need to log the shot, update the score and change the style class of the clicked cell: this last step will cause an explosion graphic to appear in the cell. The code is in Figure 15-26.

```
44        gameEngine.logShot(target);
45        gameEngine.updateCurrentScore();
46        clickedTDElement.className = "targetingGridCell hit";
47
```

Above: Figure 15-26: Add this code, which is similar to the code you wrote for step 7.

Hot Tip

Save your work regularly! This has been common advice for most computing activities for decades, but people still get caught out when a program crashes and they lose hours of work.

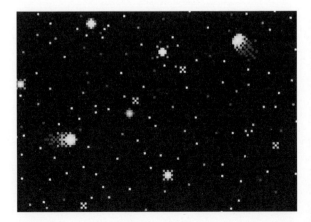

11. The Spacecraft object's getAcronym() method returns the initials of the craft's name. The DOM's innerHTML property accesses the contents of an element. Put these together, as in Figure 15-27, and we make the craft's initials appear in the clicked cell.

```
47
48          clickedTDElement.innerHTML = theSpacecraft.getAcronym();
```

Above: Figure 15-27: Add this code to make the hit spacecraft's initials show in the clicked Targeting Grid cell.

12. The Spacecraft object's takeHit() method causes the craft to register the hit. If the hit destroys the craft then takeHit() returns true, otherwise it returns false. Figure 15-28 shows the code.

```
48          var isDestroyed = theSpacecraft.takeHit(target);
49
```

Above: Figure 15-28: The Spacecraft object's takeHit() method registers the hit on the craft.

13. We need to take different actions depending on whether or not the craft has been destroyed, so we need another if statement. If destroyed we need to play the appropriate sound effect and set a suitable message: see Figure 15-29. Notice that the setMessage() method uses the concatenate operator, +, to piece together this message.

```
-49        if (isDestroyed) {
50            gameEngine.playSound("sfx_shootAndDestroy");
51            gameEngine.setMessage("Great shooting! You hit and destroyed the enemy's " + theSpacecraft.craftName + ".<br>" +
   String(gameEngine.remainingCraftCount()) + " enemy craft remaining. Keep it up!");
52
```

Above: Figure 15-29: This code will run if the enemy craft is destroyed.

14. We also need to instruct the game engine to register the destruction of the craft. The code for this is in Figure 15-30.

```
52                          gameEngine.spacecraftDestroyed();
53              }
```

Above: Figure 15-30: Register the destruction of the craft with the game engine.

15. If the craft isn't destroyed then we need to play the appropriate sound effect and set the message, as shown in Figure 15-31. Be sure that both if statements have been given a closing brace.

```
53          } else {
54              gameEngine.playSound("sfx_shootAndHit");
55              gameEngine.setMessage("Good shot. You hit enemy's " + theSpacecraft.craftName + ".<br>Try to finish it off.");
56          }
57      }
58
```

Above: Figure 15-31: Enter this code to handle what happens if the hit spacecraft isn't destroyed. Be sure to close both if statements.

16. The final thing the takeShot() function needs to do is to check if the shot has resulted in the game finishing. The game engine's gameOver property will tell us this, so we can use that as the condition to test in a new if statement.

17. The game engine's `updateBestScore()` method checks if the current score is lower (i.e. better) than the best score and, if so, it updates the stored best score value and returns `true`; otherwise it returns `false`. We'll use this to determine the message that will be shown. Figure 15-32 shows how to test and respond to the `gameOver` condition.

```
58   if (gameEngine.gameOver) {
59       var bestScoreBeaten = gameEngine.updateBestScore();
60       if (bestScoreBeaten) {
61           gameEngine.setMessage("Awesome! You've destroyed all of the alien spacecraft with a record number of shots.<br>Walk
     tall, commander.")
62       } else {
63           gameEngine.setMessage("Well done commander - you've destroyed all of the alien spacecraft.");
64       }
65   }
66
```

Above: Figure 15-32: This code handles what happens if the shot results in the game ending.

18. Save your work, open StarfleetCommand.htm in your browser, and play with your code!

SUCCESS...

Excellent work! You've done a lot of coding, and pulled off some pretty neat tricks. If things don't appear to be working properly then go back and check your code carefully for spelling mistakes, and missing semicolons, parentheses and braces. If you still can't locate the problem check your code against that contained in the Exercise 15\complete\ folder of the downloadable code package.

EXERCISE 16: **HUNGRY MAN**

Hungry Man wants to eat your lunch, the greedy guts! He's thinking of a mystery word and, if you can guess it, letter by letter, he'll let you keep your food.

ABOUT THE GAME

Hungry Man is a word guessing game. A word is selected at random from a list of over 1,000 words, and the player must try to guess the word letter by letter. Each incorrect guess sees your food move closer to Hungry Man's mouth; if it gets too close then Hungry Man will gobble it up.

CODING GOALS

In this exercise we're going to focus on the styling, and learn some new CSS tricks along the way. The HTML and JavaScript files are provided for you.

Graphics Display
Contains the Hungry Man and food graphics

Current Word
The current word to guess including any correctly guessed letters

New Game Button
Clears the current game and starts a new one

Graphics
Various graphic elements are layered together to create the finished image

Letter Buttons
The player clicks these buttons to guess a letter. The buttons change colour to indicate that they've been clicked, and whether the letter was in the current word or not

Left: The various components of the Hungry Man game screen.

STARTING POINT FILES

You'll find the starting point files for this exercise in the Exercise16\startingPoint\ folder of the downloadable code package; copy the HungryMan folder from there to a convenient working folder. You will also find a PDF of the wireframe in the Exercise 16\ folder.

Above: The wireframe for the Hungry Man game. Be sure to study it alongside the game's HTML code.

WEB FONTS

Open the HungryMan.css file in your code editor. As you will see it's empty but for one line, starting @import. This is called an import **directive**, and what it's doing is loading a web font provided by Google Fonts (fonts.google.com). To find out how to use Google Fonts visit developers.google.com/fonts/.

Above: Google Fonts has hundreds of fonts that you can use in your web pages; they even provide you with all of the code you need to use your chosen fonts.

```
1  @import url('https://fonts.googleapis.com/css?family=Khula:400,600,700,800');
```

Above: This @import directive loads a font from Google Fonts.

SETTING UP THE BASIC STYLING

1. We'll start by setting a nice background color for the page. Add a body selector and type the following in its style rule:

```
background-color: rgb(58,
73, 85);
```

```
 2
▾3  body {
 4      background-color: rgb(58, 73, 85);
 5      color: rgb(230, 230, 230);
 6      font-family: 'Khula', 'Arial', sans-serif;
 7  }
 8
```

Above: Figure 16-1: Create the body selector and style rule.

2. We'll also set the text color and font-family style properties in the body style rule so that they cascade through the rest of the document. The code is shown in Figure 16-1; notice that the font-family value includes the name of our imported web font.

```
 12
▾13  header h1 {
 14      font-size: 72px;
 15      text-align: center;
 16      margin: 10px auto 0px auto;
 17      font-weight: 800;
 18  }
 19
▾20  header p {
 21      width: 720px;
 22      margin: 0px auto 10px auto;
 23      text-align: center;
 24      font-size: 16px;
 25  }
 26
```

Above: Figure 16-2: Apply this styling to the text elements that appear in the page's <header>.

3. Add the code show in Figure 16-2 to style the text elements inside the <header>. You'll notice there are four values following each margin property; we'll explain this in a moment.

4. We want the <main> element to fill the page's width, but also need a bit of margin around it, and for it to sit centrally on the page. The code in Figure 16-3 will do this for us.

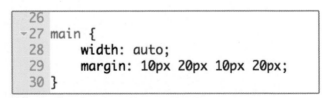

```
 26
▾27  main {
 28      width: auto;
 29      margin: 10px 20px 10px 20px;
 30  }
```

Above: Figure 16-3: Enter this code for styling the <main> element.

5. We want the `<footer>` to centrally align its `<button>` element; this is an inline element and so can be centralized with the text-align property. We'll also give `<footer>` a bit of a gap from `<main>`. Add the code in Figure 16-4 to your style sheet, then save the document.

```
31
32  footer {
33      text-align: center;
34      padding-top: 10px;
35  }
36
```

Above: Figure 16-4: Style the page's `<footer>` like this.

MULTIPLE MARGIN VALUES

The `margin` style property can take a value consisting of four measurements. Each measurement corresponds to one side of the element's box, in the order: top, right, bottom, left (i.e. they run clockwise from the top). This is just shorthand for the individual properties `margin-top`, `margin-right`, and so on.

> **Hot Tip**
>
> The technique for giving multiple `margin` values also works for `padding` and for the various border **properties**.

CENTRALIZING ELEMENTS USING MARGINS

Take a look at the style rules for the text elements in the `<header>`. Both declare a `text-align: center;` property, but this only centralizes the text within the text element's box; it doesn't centralize the text element within its containing element. To do this we use a little trick with margins: if we set the left and right margins to be the same value then the element's box will be centralized within its containing element.

BORDER STYLING

Borders have three style properties: the `border-style` property sets whether the border is solid, dashed and so on. `border-width` sets the thickness of the border and `border-color`, unsurprisingly, sets the color of the border.

STYLING THE GRAPHICS DISPLAY AREA

1. The graphics display area has a fixed size and a visible border, is centralized on the page, and has a lighter background color than the rest of the page. Also, we don't want the graphics inside the display area to be visible when they overshoot the area. The code for this is shown in Figure 16-5.

```
32
33 #graphicsDisplayWrapper {
34     width: 720px;
35     height: 405px;
36     border-style: solid;
37     border-width: 1px;
38     border-color: rgb(230, 230, 230);
39     margin: 20px auto 10px auto;
40     background-color: rgb(89, 112, 130);
41     overflow: hidden;
42 }
43
```

Above: Figure 16-5: Style the Graphics Display area with this selector and style rule.

2. The graphics inside the display will use absolute positioning so they can be placed precisely, therefore the Graphics Display area must act as the containing element for those graphics. This means it can't use default static positioning; relative positioning with no offsets will do the trick, however, and won't change the position of the Graphics Display. So add position: relative; to the #graphicsDisplayWrapper style rule.

```
32
33 #graphicsDisplayWrapper {
34     width: 720px;
35     height: 405px;
36     border-style: solid;
37     border-width: 1px;
38     border-color: rgb(230, 230, 230);
39     margin: 20px auto 10px auto;
40     background-color: rgb(89, 112, 130);
41     overflow: hidden;
42     position: relative;
43 }
44
```

Above: Figure 16-6: The completed #graphicsDisplayWrapper style rule.

3. When created by JavaScript, all game graphics are given a style class of "gameGraphic", so we can use this to target those elements with a Class selector. The code is shown in Figure 16-7.

```
44
45 #graphicsDisplayWrapper .gameGraphic {
46     position: absolute;
47     transition-duration: 1s;
48     transition-timing-function: ease-in-out;
49 }
50
```

Above: Figure 16-7: This Descendant selector targets the graphics that make up Hungry Man's face, tongue, hand and food.

4. While we're here, we'll style the other two wrapper elements. The code is shown in Figure 16-8, and should be familiar. Save your work when done.

```
50
51 #currentWordWrapper {
52     height: 70px;
53     width: auto;
54     margin: 10px 0px 10px 0px;
55 }
56
57 #letterButtonsWrapper {
58     width: auto;
59     height: 100px;
60     margin: 30px 0px 10px 0px;
61 }
62
```

Above: Figure 16-8: Style the remaining two wrapper elements.

CSS ANIMATION

The transition-duration property you've just entered lies at the heart of CSS's animation abilities. The value of 1s means that any changes made to an animatable property, such as a position offset property or color value, will be made gradually over a period of one second.

Hot Tip

Animation was introduced in CSS3, the third update to the language. All current mainstream browsers support CSS3.

The `transition-timing-function` property ramps the animation to make it smoother and more natural. The upshot of this for our game graphics is that when the player makes an incorrect guess, and the game's scripts set Hungry Man's hand and food to be closer to his mouth, the movement is animated for us.

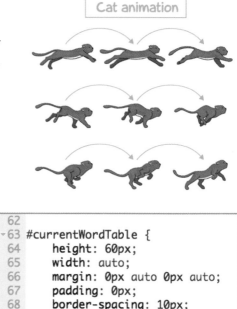

Cat animation

ADDING THE REST OF THE STYLING

1. The secret word being guessed is displayed as a single-row table; the styling for that table is shown in Figure 16-9. The only new thing here is the `border-spacing` property, which controls the space between the cells of a table.

```
62
63  #currentWordTable {
64      height: 60px;
65      width: auto;
66      margin: 0px auto 0px auto;
67      padding: 0px;
68      border-spacing: 10px;
69  }
70
```

Above: Figure 16-9: This code styles the table which represents the hidden word.

2. JavaScript creates a `<td>` element for each letter in the secret word; the styling is shown in Figure 16-10. Notice how the underlines for each letter are created using the bottom border of each `<td>`.

```
70
71  #currentWordTable td {
72      border-bottom: solid;
73      border-bottom-width: 2px;
74      border-bottom-color: rgb(230, 230, 230);
75      color: rgb(230, 230, 230);
76      width: 40px;
77      height: 60px;
78      text-align: center;
79      font-size: 48px;
80      line-height: 100%;
81      vertical-align: middle;
82  }
83
```

Above: Figure 16-10: Add this script for styling the cells of the hidden word's table.

3. Each letter button is a `<button>` element, and these are arranged in two rows, each row being a `<div>`. The styling for both is shown in Figure 16-11. New here is the `border-radius` property, which rounds the corners of an element's border box.

```
 83
 84 #letterButtonsWrapper div {
 85     margin: 0px auto 0px auto;
 86     padding: 0px;
 87     text-align: center;
 88 }
 89
 90 #letterButtonsWrapper button {
 91     width: 36px;
 92     height: 36px;
 93     border-radius: 5px;
 94     border-style: none;
 95     color: rgb(230, 230, 230);
 96     font-size: 18px;
 97     font-weight: 400;
 98     text-align: center;
 99     margin: 5px;
100     transition-duration: 0.5s;
101 }
102
```

Above: Figure 16-11: Enter this code to style the buttons which the user clicks to guess a letter.

Hot Tip

The `vertical-align` property is a table-specific style property that vertically positions the contents of a `<td>` element.

4. The color of the letter buttons indicates whether they've been tried yet, and whether that try was successful. JavaScript controls this by changing the style class of each `<button>` element as needed. The styling for those classes is shown in Figure 16-12.

```
102
103 #letterButtonsWrapper button.untried {
104     background-color: rgb(70, 119, 200);
105     color: rgb(230, 230, 230);
106 }
107
108 #letterButtonsWrapper button.nomatch {
109     background-color: rgb(135, 135, 135);
110 }
111
112 #letterButtonsWrapper button.match {
113     background-color: rgb(70, 200, 75);
114 }
115
```

Above: Figure 16-12: These selectors style the different states of the letter buttons.

5. We want untried letter buttons to change color when the mouse is over them. To do this we use the :hover Pseudo-Class selector, as shown in Figure 16-13. The cursor property here changes the mouse cursor to a finger pointer.

```
·116 #letterButtonsWrapper button.untried:hover {
 117     background-color: rgb(15, 107, 255);
 118     color: rgb(255, 255, 255);
 119     cursor: pointer;
 120 }
```

Above: Figure 16-13: Add this Pseudo-Class selector and style rule (*see* Pseudo-Class selectors on page 117).

6. The styling for the New Game button is shown in Figure 16-14. You should by now understand everything in the style rule.

```
·122 #newGameButton {
 123     font-size: 18px;
 124     font-weight: 400;
 125     color: rgb(230, 230, 230);
 126     background-color: rgb(70, 119, 200);
 127     width: auto;
 128     padding: 6px 20px 6px 20px;
 129     margin: 4px 10px 4px 10px;
 130     border-radius: 10px;
 131     border-style: none;
 132     transition-duration: 0.5s;
 133 }
 134
·135 #newGameButton:hover {
 136     cursor: pointer;
 137     color: rgb(255, 255, 255);
 138     background-color: rgb(15, 107, 255);
 139 }
```

Above: Figure 16-14: Add this code into your style sheet.

7. When the game finishes, a message panel is displayed reporting the outcome of the game. The code in Figure 16-15 styles this panel.

```
 140
·141 #gameOverMessage {
 142     position: absolute;
 143     width:700px;
 144     height:auto;
 145     text-align: center;
 146     top: 110px;
 147     margin: 0px;
 148     padding: 10px 10px 10px 10px;
 149     background-color: rgba(0, 0, 0, 0.5);
 150 }
```

Above: Figure 16-15: Enter the code that will style the Game Over message.

8. Finally, the styling for the Game Over message's text elements is shown in Figure 16-16. Save your work once you've entered this code.

Right: Figure 16-16: Add this code and then save the style sheet.

```
·152 #gameOverMessage h2 {
 153     color:rgb(255, 255, 255);
 154     font-weight: 800;
 155     font-size: 48px;
 156     text-align: center;
 157     margin: 5px;
 158 }
 159
·160 #gameOverMessage p {
 161     color: rgb(255, 255, 255);
 162     font-size:18px;
 163     width: 500px;
 164     height: auto;
 165     text-align: center;
 166     margin: 5px auto 5px auto;
 167 }
```

GREAT WORK!

Launch HungryMan.htm in your web browser, start a game and enjoy the results of your hard work.

EXPERIMENTING WITH STYLING

You can play around with the styling of a page from within most web browsers. In Firefox, open the Tools menu, and select Toggle Tools from the Web Developer menu item (other browsers have similar options). This opens an Inspector panel that shows the HTML of your page. Clicking on an element shows its styling in a side panel, from where you can add and remove style properties, and change their values, while seeing the results onscreen immediately. It's a fantastic way to experiment with and hone the design of a page. Take the time to play around with this tool and become familiar with its abilities. It's phenomenally helpful.

Above: Your web browser's code inspector is a great way to experiment with a page's styling.

EXERCISE 17: **CODEBREAKER**

In CodeBreaker, the player has to guess a hidden code. The code is a sequence of graphic symbols, and the player can choose the length of the hidden code, the number of symbols the game uses, and the maximum number of guesses allowed. Depending on settings, there are between 1,296 and 100,000,000 possible code combinations.

AIMS OF THIS EXERCISE

The aim of this exercise, other than giving you a fun game to play, is to introduce you to some new elements of all three web languages, and to show you some nifty little tricks along the way.

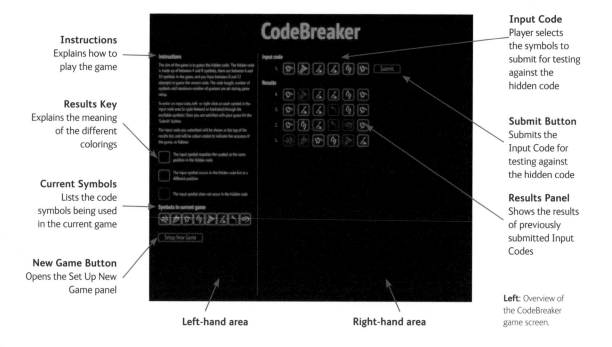

Instructions
Explains how to play the game

Results Key
Explains the meaning of the different colorings

Current Symbols
Lists the code symbols being used in the current game

New Game Button
Opens the Set Up New Game panel

Input Code
Player selects the symbols to submit for testing against the hidden code

Submit Button
Submits the Input Code for testing against the hidden code

Results Panel
Shows the results of previously submitted Input Codes

Left-hand area   **Right-hand area**

Left: Overview of the CodeBreaker game screen.

Exercise Files

The starting point files for this exercise are in the Exercise17\startingPoint\ folder of the downloadable code package: copy these to a convenient working folder location. The wireframes for the page design are also in the Exercise17\ folder.

BACKGROUND IMAGES

As well as being able to set an element's background color, we can also assign an image to appear in the element's background. This was the method used for displaying the explosion graphics in the Starfleet Command game. Adding a single image in that way is one use of background images, but CodeBreaker uses them for a full screen background fill.

Gradient Fills

If you look closely at the CodeBreaker screen you will see that the background color of the page is a gradient that goes from black at the top of the screen to dark blue at the bottom. This is done using an image file of a color gradient. But surely an image file that fills the screen would be quite large and so unsuitable for use over the internet? So how do we do it?

Above: Wireframe of the CodeBreaker game.

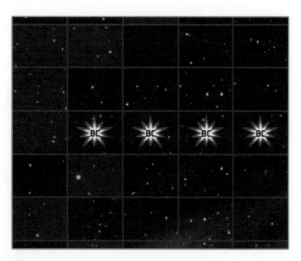

Above: In Starfleet Command, the explosion graphics are applied as background images of the `<td>` elements in the Targeting Grid.

CREATING CODEBREAKER'S COLOR GRADIENT BACKGROUND

1. Open your graphics editor and create a new document that's 10 pixels wide and 768 pixels high. You need to fill the image with a linear color gradient that goes from black to dark blue; the dark blue color should be red: 0, green: 12, blue: 32.

2. How you create this gradient will depend on the graphics editor you are using; in Affinity Designer or Adobe Illustrator, for example, you would create a rectangle that filled the image, give the rectangle a transparent stroke color, and then use the Fill tool to create the color gradient as the rectangle's fill color. If you don't know how to do this in your editor then consult its Help pages or manual.

Above: In your image editor create a new image that's 10 x 768 pixels in size.

Right: Affinity Designer's Fill tool lets you create gradient fills in moments.

3. Save the image as a PNG file in your CodeBreaker\img\ folder; name the file bg.png. (If you have trouble completing these steps then you can copy the bg.png file from the Exercise17\complete\ folder in the downloadable code package.)

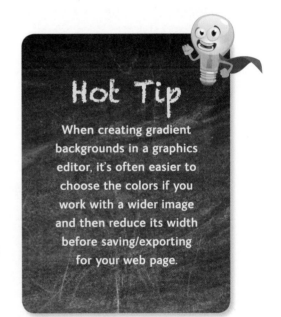

Above: Save the image in your CodeBreaker project's img folder as bg.png.

4. Open CodeBreaker.css in your code editor (it's in the project's css subfolder). At the top of the document add a body selector.

5. To set the image we use the `background-image` style property, as shown in Figure 17-1. This uses a URL to point to the image we want to use. That URL has to be relative to the CSS file, not the HTML file, but because the image file is not in the css subfolder (or a subfolder of it) we need to back out of the css subfolder so we can go into the img subfolder. The " . . / " section of the URL value is what does this: it means go back to the current folder's parent folder.

Hot Tip

When creating gradient backgrounds in a graphics editor, it's often easier to choose the colors if you work with a wider image and then reduce its width before saving/exporting for your web page.

```
1 body {
2       background-image: url("../img/bg.png");
3 }
4
```

Above: Figure 17-1: Add this code to the CodeBreaker.css style sheet.

```
3    background-position: 0px 0px;
4    background-repeat: repeat-x;
```

Above: Figure 17-2: This code positions the background image and tells it to repeat across the screen.

6. We want our gradient image to be fixed to the upper-left corner of the `<body>` element (i.e. the page's visible area), and to be repeated across the element. The code in Figure 17-2 does this – add it to the `body` selector's style rule.

Hot Tip

Generally speaking, background images should be quite subtle and understated; if you use too much color, contrast or brightness then they can interfere with the legibility of the page content.

7. The `background-attachment` style property determines

```
5    background-attachment: fixed;
```

Above: Figure 17-3: This code makes the background image remain static on the page.

whether the background image scrolls with the page or not. In this instance we want it to remain static – add the code in Figure 17-3 to your `body` style rule to achieve this.

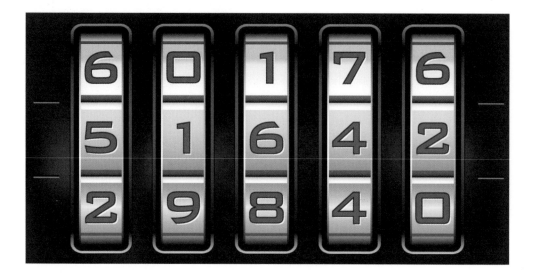

8. The gradient graphic is 768 pixels high; if the page is taller than this then, as things stand, we'd see a default white background color below the bottom of the gradient. Setting the background color to match the end color of the gradient will sort this out. Save your work once you've added the code shown in Figure 17-4 to your body selector.

| 6 | background-color: rgb(0, 12, 32); |

Above: Figure 17-4: Set the background color so that it blends with the end of the gradient.

Hot Tip

Use popups with care. If you use too many you will annoy visitors to your page.

POPUPS

It's quite common for web pages to feature popup windows. CodeBreaker features two such popups: one to gather setup info at the beginning of the game, and one to report at the end of the game. Let's take a look.

Game Over

Success!

There were 262,144 possible combinations for the hidden code, and you cracked it in 7 tries.

Setup New Game

Above: CodeBreaker's Game Over popup.

CREATING THE GAME OVER POPUP

1. Open CodeBreaker.htm in your code editor. Scroll down through the document to find the `<section id="rightPanel">` element and then below and outside of this element, but still within `<main>`, add the code shown in Figure 17-5, and then save the document.

Above: Wireframe of the Game Over popup panel.

```
81
82    <section id="gameOverPanel">
83        <h2>Game Over</h2>
84        <div id="gameOverMessage"></div>
85        <button onclick="showGameSetupPanel();">Setup New Game</button>
86    </section>
87
```

Above: Figure 17-5: Add this code after the closing tag of the `<section>` element containing the page's right-hand panel.

2. Open CodeBreaker.css in your editor and create a `#gameOverPanel` ID selector.

3. We want to position the panel relative to the web browser window so in the `#gameOverPanel` style rule add `position: fixed;` (see Positioning Modes on page 147).

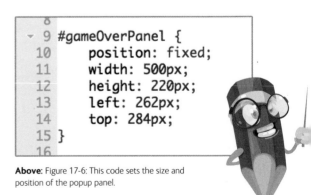

```
8
9  #gameOverPanel {
10      position: fixed;
11      width: 500px;
12      height: 220px;
13      left: 262px;
14      top: 284px;
15 }
16
```

Above: Figure 17-6: This code sets the size and position of the popup panel.

4. The panel needs to be 500 pixels wide and 220 pixels high; it needs to be 262 pixels from the left of the browser window, and 284 pixels below the top edge. The whole style rule is shown in Figure 17-6.

5. The visual styling of the popup's element box is shown in Figure 17-7. We're also including the `text-align` property to centre the popup's `<button>` element.

```
15        background-color: rgb(0, 0, 0);
16        border-style: solid;
17        border-width: 1px;
18        border-color: rgb(74, 165, 247);
19        text-align: center;
```

Above: Figure 17-7: Apply some element box styling to the Game Over popup.

6. We want the popup panel to remain hidden until we need it so add `display: none;` to the style rule and then save your work. There are other styles controlling the popup's elements; you can study these in the CodeBreakerPrebuilt.css file.

```
 8
 9 #gameOverPanel {
10        position: fixed;
11        width: 500px;
12        height: 220px;
13        left: 262px;
14        top: 284px;
15        background-color: rgb(0, 0, 0);
16        border-style: solid;
17        border-width: 1px;
18        border-color: rgb(74, 165, 247);
19        text-align: center;
20        display: none;
21 }
22
```

Above: The finished `#gameOverPanel` style rule should look like this.

7. Open gameControl.js from within your project's js subfolder. Scroll down to the bottom of the script where you'll find a function declaration for `reportGameOver()`. The function's parameter, `gameStatus`, expects a String value of either `"won"` or `"lost"`.

```
 99
100 function reportGameOver(gameStatus) {
101        var gameOverPanel = document.getElementById("gameOverPanel");
102
103 }
104
```

Above: Figure 17-8: This code gets a reference to the Game Over panel's element: add it to your script.

8. We want to get hold of the Game Over panel so that we can do things with it; the `getElementById()` method of the `document` object will do this for us. This is shown in Figure 17-8 (*see* previous page).

8. The panel displays a message within the `<div id="gameOverMessage">` element. Figure 17-9 shows how to get a reference to that element.

Hot Tip

If you're curious about how the game engine calculates the values it returns to your scripts then open up the CodeBreaker. js script, locate the method definitions and see for yourself.

```
102    var messageElement = document.getElementById("gameOverMessage");
103
```

Above: Figure 17-9: Add this code to get a reference to the `<div>` where the Game Over message will be displayed.

10. The game engine's `getNumberOfPossibleCodes()` method calculates the number of possible code variations in the game; this number is included in the message shown in the popup, so for convenience let's grab it and store it in a variable. We'll do the same with the `getCurrentGuessCount()` method, which counts how many guesses the player has made in the game (*see* Figure 17-10, below).

```
103    var numberOfPossibleCodes = gameEngine.getNumberOfPossibleCodes();
104    var currentGuessCount = gameEngine.getCurrentGuessCount();
105
```

Above: Figure 17-10: Enter these statements in order to get from the game engine the values that are needed for the Game Over message.

```
106    if (gameStatus == "won") {
107        var messageText = "Success!<br><br>There were " + numberOfPossibleCodes.toLocaleString() +
" possible combinations for the hidden code, and you cracked it in " + currentGuessCount + " tries.";
108    }
109
```

Above: Figure 17-11: This `if` statement will create an appropriate message if the game is won.

11. The message will differ depending on whether the game was won or lost, so we'll generate the message within an `if` statement that tests the condition of `gameStatus`.

12. We're going to use the concatenate operator to build up the message. When adding the `numberOfPossibleCodes` value, a Number object, to the message we're using the `toLocaleString()` method of the Number class, which converts a number to a String object and places commas in the string to make it easier to read. The code is in Figure 17-11 on the previous page.

```
108      } else {
109          var messageText = "You failed to crack the code!<br><br>There were " + numberOfPossibleCodes
        + " possible combinations for the hidden code.";
110      }
```

Above: Figure 17-12: This `else` clause creates an appropriate message if the game is lost.

13. The message will need to be different if the game was lost – we can handle this in an `else` clause, as shown in Figure 17-12 above.

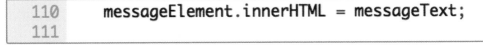

```
110        messageElement.innerHTML = messageText;
111
```

Above: Figure 17-13: Add this statement to your script.

14. Now it's generated we can assign the message to the `<div id="gameOverMessage">` element; we can do this using its `innerHTML` property: *see* Figure 17-13, which should be written after the if statement.

```
111        gameOverPanel.style.display = "block";
112 }
```

Above: Figure 17-14: Finally, enter this statement to make the Game Over popup visible.

15. Finally, we want to display the Game Over popup. We can refer to the popup panel element using the `gameOverPanel` variable. Setting the `style.display` property of that element to `block` will apply a `display: block;` style property to the panel, making it visible. Enter the code shown in Figure 17-14 and then save your work.

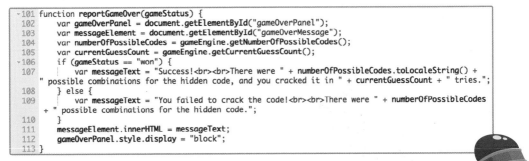

```
101 function reportGameOver(gameStatus) {
102     var gameOverPanel = document.getElementById("gameOverPanel");
103     var messageElement = document.getElementById("gameOverMessage");
104     var numberOfPossibleCodes = gameEngine.getNumberOfPossibleCodes();
105     var currentGuessCount = gameEngine.getCurrentGuessCount();
106     if (gameStatus == "won") {
107         var messageText = "Success!<br><br>There were " + numberOfPossibleCodes.toLocaleString() +
    " possible combinations for the hidden code, and you cracked it in " + currentGuessCount + " tries.";
108     } else {
109         var messageText = "You failed to crack the code!<br><br>There were " + numberOfPossibleCodes
    + " possible combinations for the hidden code.";
110     }
111     messageElement.innerHTML = messageText;
112     gameOverPanel.style.display = "block";
113 }
```

Above: The entire `reportGameOver()` function should look like this.

DROPDOWN MENUS

Our other popup panel contains three dropdown menus; these are created using `<select>` elements. Those elements (and their labels) are arranged in a table. Let's set that up.

Above: Wireframe for the Game Setup panel.

Hot Tip

We could lay out the Game Setup panel using `<div>` elements styled to create a table-like layout, but these layouts are quicker to create with a `<table>` element.

USING DROPDOWN MENUS

1. Open CodeBreaker.htm in your code editor. Scroll down the document and create an empty line below the `<section id="gameOverPanel">`. Create a new `<section>` with an `id` attribute value of `"gameSetupPanel"`.

2. Add an `<h2>` heading containing the text `"Game Setup"`.

3. Create a new `<table>` element with a `<tbody>` element within it (*see* Figure 17-15).

```
87
88    <section id="gameSetupPanel">
89        <h2>Game Setup</h2>
90        <table>
91            <tbody>
92
93            </tbody>
94        </table>
95    </section>
96
```

Above: Figure 17-15: Create a `<section>` element for the Game Setup panel underneath the Game Over panel's closing tag.

4. Add the first `<tr>` row to the `<tbody>` element. Add a `<td>` within this and give it a `class` attribute value of `"optionTitle"`. Put the text `"Number of Symbols"` within the `<td>` (*see* Figure 17-16).

Above: Figure 17-16: Create a row in the table's body, and create a cell in that row, using this code.

```
92    <tr>
93        <td class="optionTitle">Number of symbols</td>
94
95    </tr>
96
```

```
 94      <td>
 95         <select id="numSymbolsOption">
 96            <option value="6">6</option>
 97            <option value="7">7</option>
 98            <option value="8">8</option>
 99            <option value="9">9</option>
100            <option value="10">10</option>
101         </select>
102      </td>
```

Above: Figure 17-17: The second cell in the row contains the dropdown menu itself – this is its code.

5. Add a second `<td>` element within the `<tr>` row.

6. Add a `<select>` element inside the second `<td>`; give the `<select>` an `id` attribute value of `"numSymbolsOption"`. `<select>` creates a dropdown menu; the entries in the menu are listed in `<option>` elements within the `<select>` element. The actual value of each option (as opposed to the text displayed in the popup, which can be different from the value) is set as an attribute of each `<option>` element. The full code is shown in Figure 17-17.

```
104   <tr>
105      <td class="optionTitle">Code length:</td>
106      <td>
107         <select id="codeLengthOption">
108            <option value="4">4</option>
109            <option value="5">5</option>
110            <option value="6">6</option>
111            <option value="7">7</option>
112            <option value="8">8</option>
113         </select>
114      </td>
115   </tr>
```

Above: Figure 17-18: Create the second row of the `<table>` element.

7. The next table row will have a similar form. This row determines the length of the hidden word the player has to guess. Add the HTML code shown in Figure 17-18.

```
116   <tr>
117       <td class="optionTitle">Maximum guesses:</td>
118       <td>
119           <select id="maxGuessesOption">
120               <option value="8">8</option>
121               <option value="9">9</option>
122               <option value="10">10</option>
123               <option value="11">11</option>
124               <option value="12">12</option>
125           </select>
126       </td>
127   </tr>
```

Above: Figure 17-19: The table's third row is created with this code.

8. The last table row sets the maximum number of guesses allowed. The code is shown in Figure 17-19.

```
130
131       <button onclick="startGame();">Start Game</button>
132
```

Above: Figure 17-20: Add the `<button>` element that will call the `startGame()` function when clicked.

9. Add the Start Game button underneath the table, as shown in Figure 17-20, and then save the HTML document.

10. Open CodeBreaker.css. Locate the `#gameOverPanel` selector. The styling for the Game Setup is the same as this, so add the `#gameSetupPanel` selector as a multiple ID selector: *see* Figure 17-21.

11. Save the style sheet and then open gameControl.js from the project's js subfolder. Find the declaration for the (currently empty) `showGameSetupPanel()` function.

```
8
9  #gameOverPanel, #gameSetupPanel {
10     position: fixed;
11     width: 500px;
12     height: 220px;
13     left: 262px;
14     top: 284px;
15     background-color: rgb(0, 0, 0);
16     border-style: solid;
17     border-width: 1px;
18     border-color: rgb(74, 165, 247);
19     text-align: center;
20     display: none;
21 }
22
```

Above: Figure 17-21: Add an additional ID selector after the `#gameOverPanel` selector; don't forget to put a comma between the two selectors.

```
27
28  function showGameSetupPanel() {
29      document.getElementById("gameOverPanel").style.display = "none";
30      document.getElementById("setupNewGameButton").style.display = "none";
31
```

Above: Figure 17-22: Add these statements to hide elements that shouldn't be visible when the Game Setup panel is visible.

12. showGameSetupPanel() will generally be called from the Game Over panel, so we can assume that panel is visible when the function is called. Also, there's a Setup New Game button always present on the screen, which shouldn't be present whilst the Game Setup panel is visible. The code in Figure 17-22 will deal with both these things.

```
31      document.getElementById("gameSetupPanel").style.display = "block";
32
```

Above: Figure 17-23: Add this statement to make the Game Over panel visible.

13. To show the Game Setup panel, we just need to set its display style property to block; the code is in Figure 17-23.

```
39
40  function startGame() {
41      document.getElementById("gameSetupPanel").style.display = "none";
42      document.getElementById("setupNewGameButton").style.display = "inline";
43
44  }
45
```

Above: Figure 17-24: Add this code to the startGame() function.

14. Locate the declaration for the startGame() function. The first thing this function must do is hide the Game Setup panel and show the Start New Game button again on the main game screen. The code is in Figure 17-24 and should be familiar.

15. The values the player selected in the dropdown menus are available as the value attribute of each <select> element. Figure 17-25 shows you how to store those values in variables.

```
43    var numSymbols = document.getElementById("numSymbolsOption").value;
44    var codeLength = document.getElementById("codeLengthOption").value;
45    var maxGuesses = document.getElementById("maxGuessesOption").value;
46
```

Above: Figure 17-25: Enter these statements to get the values the player entered in the Game Setup panel.

16. Finally, we need to pass the values to the game engine's startNewGame() method. Enter the code in Figure 17-26 and then save your work.

```
46        gameEngine.startNewGame(numSymbols, codeLength, maxGuesses);
47 }
48
```

Above: Figure 17-26: Finally, enter this statement, which will start the game using the game settings entered by the player.

BREAK THE CODE

Launch CodeBreaker.htm in your web browser and bask in the glory of all of that determined effort!

HAPPY CODING

We've covered an awful lot of ground in this book, but so far, you've only taken your first steps into the world of web programming. There's an awful lot more to find out about, and a lot more tricks and techniques to learn. Rereading this book should bring new insights, as will studying the code supplied with the game projects. On the next few pages you will also find some suggested websites and books that will help you to progress further. Happy coding!

USEFUL WEBSITES

There are a huge number of websites and channels dedicated to helping people improve their coding prowess. Some act like reference sites, others provide step-by-step tutorials, some do both.

W3SCHOOLS.COM

w3schools.com (www.w3schools.com) is a great site for web developers. It covers most web-related technologies, not just HTML, CSS and JavaScript, but frameworks such as JQuery and Bootstrap too. The site features easy-to-access reference information, which includes example code and browser compatibility information – invaluable when you need to remind yourself how an element or class works. It also offers many detailed tutorials to help you fill the gaps in your knowledge.

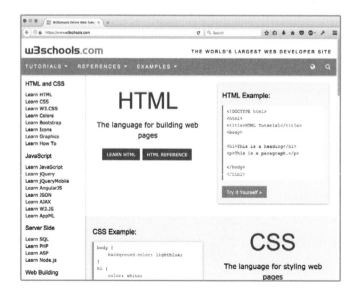

Left: w3schools.com contains loads of invaluable reference and tutorial content.

Hot Tip

Frameworks are pre-written code libraries that sit between your code and the web page, providing helpers and functionality that simplifies the development process.

YOUTUBE

Video explainers, if done well, can be much easier to understand than long passages of text, especially when dealing with complicated or fiddly concepts such as binary and hexadecimal numbering (something that all developers need to have an understanding of). YouTube and other video sites contain a lot of such material, so don't neglect to search there for coding lessons and tutorials.

WORLD WIDE WEB CONSORTIUM (W3C)

The W3C (www.w3.org) are the official arbiters of the technologies that are used on the web. When people talk about web standards, what they are referring to are the guidelines and white papers issued by the W3C. There's a lot of dry and highly technical discussion on the site, but there's a lot of very accessible material too. Ultimately, the W3C is the place to visit if you want to learn all there is to know about an aspect of web technology.

Left: The World Wide Web Consortium set the standards for web technology. The info on their site, therefore, is pretty much the first and last word on everything to do with the web.

FURTHER READING

Most developers have at least one shelf in their office stacked with books on programming and development. Some are huge tomes with hundreds of pages of dense text, others are designed to be more accessible. All are useful!

OTHER BOOKS BY THE SAME AUTHOR

Flame Tree Publishing also publish *Coding HTML, CSS and JavaScript*, by the author of *Coding for Kids*. In the first half of the book, co-written with Frederic Johnson, the reader is given an easy-to-use and practical guide to programming in HTML and CSS. The second half of the book is dedicated to JavaScript, and digs into the fundamentals of the language, explaining them with clear diagrams and examples.

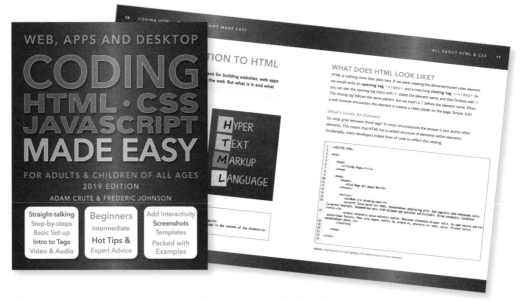

Above: This book by the same author gives more detail on the topics covered in *Coding for Kids*.

OTHER RECOMMENDED BOOKS

Harold, E. R., and Means, W. S., *XML in a Nutshell*, O'Reilly, 2004.
You can't get far in coding JavaScript before you encounter XML, and this book is the perfect way to get up to speed on the subject.

Hatter, Clyde, *CoderDojo: Build Your Own Website*, Egmont, 2016.
CoderDojo is a great computer club that co-exists with this book. It lets you talk to other kids interested in coding. If you want to focus on making the perfect website in a fun and social way this is the book for you.

McGrath, Mike, *Coding for Beginners in Easy Steps*, In Easy Steps Limited, 2015.
A really great introduction to coding that is part of a series that also has books specifically focusing on HTML5, CSS3 and JavaScript if you want to delve deeper into any of these languages.

Niederst Robbins, J., *HTML5 Pocket Reference*, O'Reilly, 2013.
A more advanced book that is the perfect quick-reference for HTML5 coding.

Sweigart, Al, *Invent Your Own Computer Games with Python*, No Starch Press, 2017.
This book is a great introduction to the popular programming language – Python. It's a great introduction to it, with lots more games to build.

Vorderman, Carol, *Computer Coding for Kids*, DK Children, 2014.
This book will also take you through the very basics of coding and give you some more nifty projects to try your hand at.

Woodcock, Jon, *Coding in Scratch: Projects Workbook*, DK Publishing, 2016.
This is a great book if you would like more ideas for creating animations, games and short films.

INDEX